NEW YC
FOR TOUI

The Traveler's Guide to Make The Most Out of Your Trip to New York - *Where to Go, Eat,* Sleep & Party

By Dagny Taggart

Disclaimer

The information provided in this book is designed to provide helpful information on the subjects discussed. The author's books are only meant to provide the reader with the basics travel guidelines of a certain location, without any warranties regarding the accuracy of the information and advice provided. Each traveler should do their own research before departing

Table of Contents

Dedicated to those who love going beyond their own frontiers.

Keep on traveling,

Dagny Taggart

My FREE Gift to You!

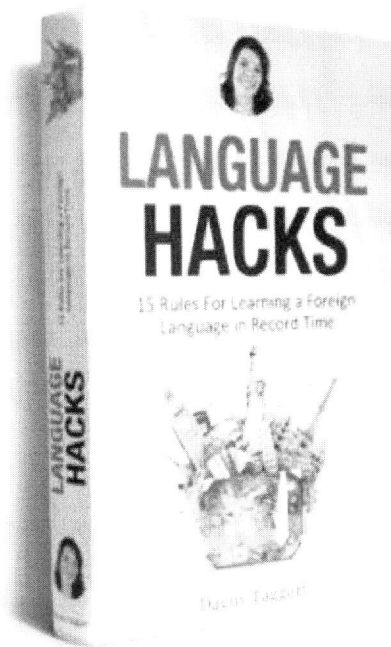

As a way of saying thank you for downloading my book, I'd like to send you an exclusive gift that will revolutionize the way you learn new languages. It's an extremely comprehensive PDF with 15 language hacking rules that **will help you learn 300% <u>faster</u>, with <u>less effort</u>, and with <u>higher than ever retention rates</u>**.

This guide is an amazing complement to the book you just got, and could easily be a stand-alone product, but for now I've decided to give it away for free, to thank you for being such an awesome reader, and to make sure I give you all the value that I can to help you succeed faster on your language learning journey.

To get your FREE gift, click on the link or the button below, follow the steps, and I'll send it to your email address right away.

>> http://bitly.com/Language-Gift <<

GET **INSTANT** ACCESS

Learn Any Language 300% FASTER

>> Get Full Online Language Courses With Audio Lessons <<

Would you like to learn a new language before you start your trip? I think that's a great idea. Now, why don't you do it 300% *FASTER*?

I've partnered with the most revolutionary language teachers to bring you the very language online courses I've ever seen. It's a mind-blowing program specifically created for language hackers such as ourselves. It will allow you learn ANY language, from French to Chinese, 3x faster, straight from the comfort of your own home, office, or wherever you may be. It's like having an unfair advantage!

You can choose from a wide variety of languages, such as French, Spanish, Italian, German, Chinese, Portuguese, and A TON more.

Each Online Course consists of:

+ 91 Built-In Lessons
+ 33 Interactive Audio Lessons
+ 24/7 Support to Keep You Going

The program is extremely engaging, fun, and easy-going. You won't even notice you are learning a complex foreign language from scratch. And before you realize it, by the time you go through all the lessons you will officially become a truly solid speaker.

Old classrooms are a thing of the past. It's time for a revolution.

If you'd like to go the extra mile, then follow the link below, and let the revolution begin!

>> http://bitly.com/foreign-language-courses <<

CHECK OUT THE COURSE »

Introduction
Welcome to New York - It's Been Waiting For You!

If you're reading this, then you're thinking of or heading to one of the greatest cities in the entire world. New York City (aka the Big Apple) is often referred to as the "City that Never Sleeps", and it stays true to its nickname for a reason. It is the most populated city in the United States of America, known as the cultural and financial capital of the world, and is seen as a major "melting pot" due to the early twentieth century mass immigration, extreme tourism, and its global impact. New York City consists of five boroughs: "trendy" Brooklyn, "food heavy" Queens, "powerhouse" Manhattan, the cultural Bronx, and traditional Staten Island. New York City is home to many corporate offices for commerce, finance, media, art, fashion, research, technology, education, and entertainment. Additionally, it is home to the headquarters of the United Nations.

Besides its impressive resume of headquarters, commerce, Ivy League colleges, and trade, New York City has life like no other. The bright lights, hurried cabs, and bustling streets attract over 55 million tourists per year.

Any map or list can tell you the popular places to go to in New York City. You can spend hours in the Museums (which I do recommend if you have time), and not know anything else but that. However, New York City isn't just Midtown Manhattan. It's the running path along the East River or the hidden speakeasy in the Upper East Side. It's the place where those who want to make it come and give it their all. It's a city filled with opportunity, hidden gems, and activities to ensure you don't sleep while you're there. The historical sites are truly breathtaking and unforgettable. The true New York charm is a bit gritty, a bit unkempt, but full of heart. This guidebook celebrates both the traditional historic charm of the concrete jungle known, as New York City, as well as the hidden gems not the average tourist will find.

New York City is what you make it. With that, what will you choose in your time visiting? Will you head to Brooklyn, home of the "hipster", sipping fresh cold dripped coffee and talking about the latest off-Broadway play, underground band, or vintage boutique? Or, will you head to the Bronx, grab a beer with a buddy, watch the famous New York Yankees play, and eat some authentic Italian. What about strolling along one of the biggest shopping streets in the world, 5th Avenue, stopping at a gourmet deli, and dancing the night away in SoHo? What will your New York be?

This guidebook takes you to both the traditional and beyond the average tour route. A true New Yorker wrote this guidebook; one who has lived in multiple boroughs, worked in multiple neighborhoods, and drank anywhere they can find a bar after noon. Who else would give you the best knowledge of where you can find the best pastrami sandwich or martini at a moment's notice? As we've said before, this guidebook is to take you to places that interest and excite you. New York is what you make of it. It won't create your itinerary, nor will it tell you every little thing that is offered in this city. It would take years to fully understand what New York has to offer. Even those born and raised in New York wouldn't claim to have seen it all. This guidebook will be your essential pal that will nudge you along your way, your beacon in sea of fast moving locals, and your guide through transportation, hot spots, historical sites, and shopping.

But first, take it in.

Breathe in the city smog, chuckle at the angry New Yorker trying to get by you, and look up at the skyscrapers in awe. This is the home of the American Dream; the land of ideas.

I hope you like caffeine, because you're going to need it to get through all that we have to cover (and if you want to look like a real New Yorker you must have a coffee in your hand).

Here's a quick rundown of our guide for easy reference.

- **Chapter 1: A brief overview of New York City**-Historical knowledge on its boroughs and neighborhoods to give you an initial understanding of the city and its landscape.

- **Chapter 2 – Essential New York Experiences**: A brief "To Do" list of New York City's top attractions from a visitor's perspective, helping you to narrow down your list and help set your itinerary.

- **Chapter 3 – Essential New York Trip Planning**: This chapter starts with a rundown of the best of New York City, important things to consider when planning your trip, and a "To Do" list of top attractions. Whether looking for historical, famous, sights or preferring adventure with the unknown attractions, we have you covered. The weather got you down? We even have options on what to do on a rainy day!

- **Chapter 4 – Where to Sleep:** From hostiles to five star luxuries, New York City hospitality is just as diverse as the city itself. Whether staying in a penthouse or sleeping on a couch, we have options for every preference. This chapter covers it all and includes what apps to use, what websites to check out, and what places to look for specifically.

- **Chapter 5 – How to use New York City's MTA/Public Transportation:** Everyone uses public transportation. From cabs to subways to buses, we have the inside scoop on all you need to know. Before you know it, you'll be nudging people out of the way like a true New Yorker.

- **Chapter 6 - How to Travel Smart, Experience More, and Spend Less:** New York City regularly appears in the top lists of the world's most expensive cities. However, you don't need to max out three credit cards to experience the Big Apple like a local. We can't afford rent and buy shoes without cutting some corners! This chapter helps take the spending out of the stratosphere.

- **Chapter 7- Where to Shop-**Ready to shop until you drop? This Chapter provides the best shopping areas as well as great stops along the way to keep you nourished.

- **Chapter 8-Holidays in NYC-**The holidays in NYC are truly a magical time. There is something about the twinkling Christmas lights, snowy streets, and mulled wine that put anyone in a good mood. Here is our list of the best places to go and get in the holiday spirit.

- **Chapters 9-**12: An in depth look into New York City's Most Popular Neighborhoods These chapters provide great tips, details, insights, noteworthy attractions, and hidden gems in each of New York City's distinguished neighborhoods. They're packed with local tips of where to eat, drink, party, and how to experience the New York City off the beaten path

- **Chapter 9-Uptown Manhattan**

- **Chapter 10-Midtown Manhattan**

- **Chapter 11-Lower Manhattan**

- **Chapter 12-Brooklyn and Queens**

- **Chapter 13: See you in the Big Apple!** A brief conclusion and thank you.

Chapter 1
New York City At a Glance (Manhattan and Its Surroundings)

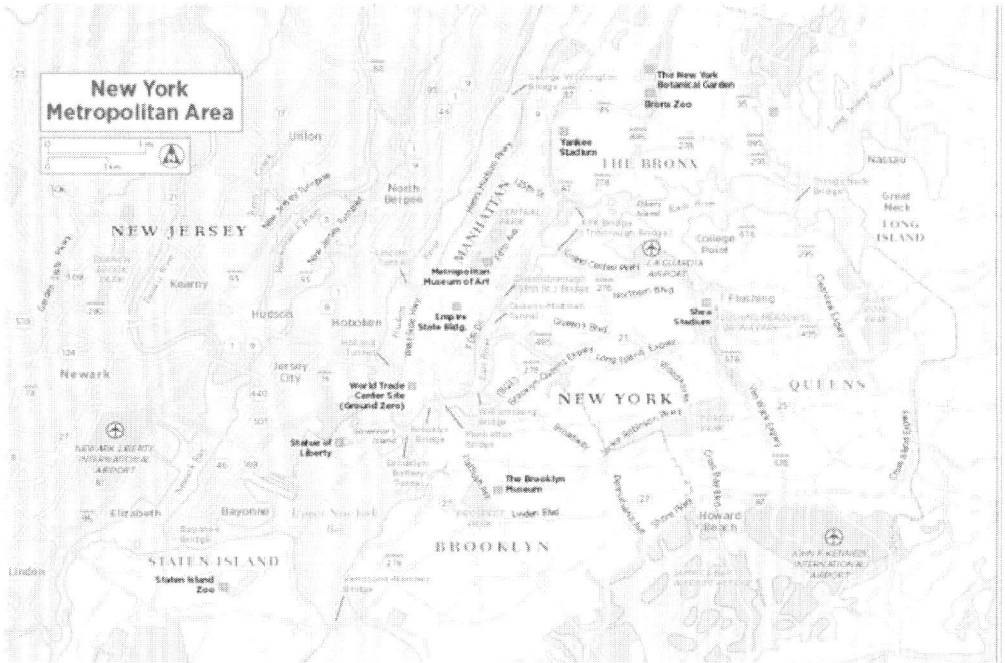

Map 1: New York City and its surrounding Boroughs

In 1609, English explorer Henry Hudson re-discovered the New York Metro region when he sailed his ship into the natural New York Harbor. Although he was searching for the Northwest Passage to the Orient, the Dutch's claim on New York City and Hudson's employer the Dutch East India Company helped New York City start to grow as an initial trading post. It wasn't until the 1700s when the British acquired the land and saw the growth potential, and invested in the land to make it a major trading port.

New York City is in the Northeastern United States. The location at the mouth of the Hudson River and along the East River, feeds into a natural sheltered harbor and then into the Atlantic Ocean. This has significantly the city grow into a major trading port. Most of New York City is built on the three islands of Long Island, Manhattan, and Staten Island.

New York City's five boroughs are home to some of the world's most recognizable, cherished landmarks and attractions. From the bright lights of Times Square to the Empire State Building and Chrysler Building to beautiful Central Park. Our prestigious museums include The Metropolitan Museum of

Art, the Museum of Modern Art, the Guggenheim, and the Museum of Natural History, among many others. The island of Manhattan packs more famous icons into one compact area than any other place on earth; and we haven't even started talking about the City's four other boroughs—The Bronx, Brooklyn, Queens and Staten Island—each of which contains its own roster of must-see destinations. With so much to see and do, a trip to NYC may seem a little overwhelming. New York's neighborhoods are each distinct with their own characteristics and personalities.

- **Manhattan Island** is the most densely populated and well-known borough. Home to Central Park, most of the city skyscrapers (including the world's tallest skyscraper), as well as all of the major shopping, theater, and arts districts. Randall's Island, Wards Island, and Roosevelt Island in the East River, and Governors Island and Liberty Island to the south in New York Harbor also reign under the Manhattan borough. Manhattan is home to most of the cultural and financial capital to New York City. It is home to many corporations, the United Nations Headquarters, universities, and many cultural attractions. Iconic scenes such as the Plaza Hotel from *Home Alone 2* or Audrey Hepburn strolling the streets in *Breakfast at Tiffany's,* or Carrie Bradshaw in *Sex and the City*, are all filmed in Manhattan.

  Manhattan Island is separated into neighborhoods that fall into the Lower, Midtown, and Uptown sections. Uptown Manhattan is divided by Central Park into the Upper East Side and the Upper West Side, and above the park is Harlem. New York City's remaining four boroughs are known as the "outer boroughs".

- **The Bronx** is home of the famous home of the New York Yankees, as well as the Bronx Zoo: the world's largest metropolitan zoo. The Bronx is also the birthplace of rap and hip-hop culture. It is known for its growing restaurant scene

- **Brooklyn** is currently one of the fastest growing areas of New York City. It's located on the western tip of Long Island. Brooklyn is known for its "hipster" culture, art scene, ethnic neighborhoods, and architectural heritage. Iconic Coney Island and their world famous hot dog competition reside at the tip of Brooklyn.

- **Queens** on Long Island east of Brooklyn is the largest borough as well as the most ethnically diverse county. Queens is home to the New York Mets and their renowned Citi Field stadium. The annual U.S. Open tennis tournament takes place in Queens. Additionally, two of the three main airports for New York City (LaGuardia Airport and John F. Kennedy International Airport), are located in Queens. (The third is Newark Liberty International Airport in Newark, New Jersey.)

- **Staten Island** is the most suburban and stereotypical (due to media) of the boroughs. The Verrazano-Narrows Bridge connects Staten Island to Brooklyn and to Manhattan by way of the free Staten Island Ferry, a daily commuter ferry (Insider's Tip: It's FREE) and popular tourist attraction, which provides unobstructed views of the Statue of Liberty, Ellis Island, and Lower Manhattan. Getting Started- Manhattan's neighborhoods

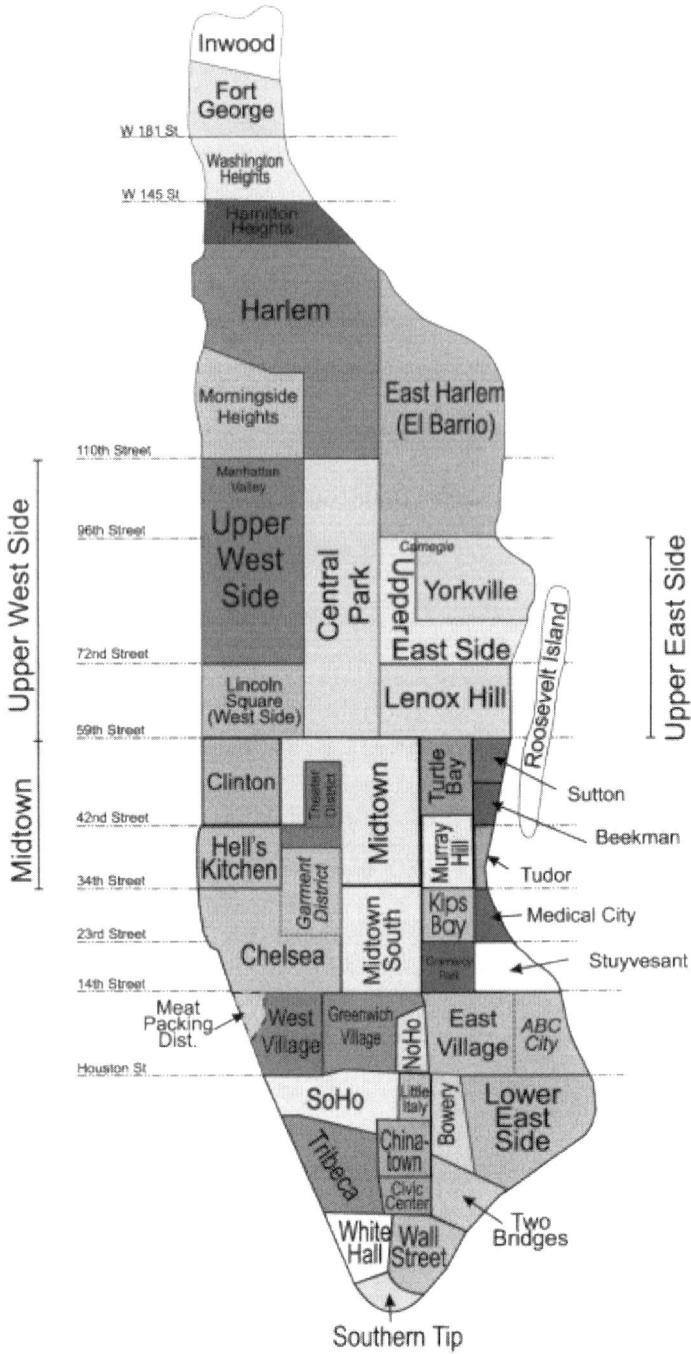

Map 2: Manhattan's Neighborhoods

Although Manhattan is smaller in comparison to Brooklyn or Queens (Brooklyn is actually three times the size of the big island!), it is a melting pot of culture and variety. The Commissioners' Plan of 1811 was the design that established Manhattan's famed street grid. The plan is well known to be called "the single most important document in New York City's Development". Although this plan was commissioned before the building of Central Park, its planned grid that uses Streets for roads East to West and Avenues from North to South is not only used today, but it's organization has been contributed to helping the city's fast growth. During this grow, many immigrants moved to certain neighborhoods due to the strong language barrier. Decades later, these neighborhoods stuck! Manhattan's diverse and largely populated area is split into distinct neighborhoods, which are separated by both architecture and culture. To truly understand New York City is to understand the neighborhoods and the history behind each.

- Uptown Manhattan-the area above 59th Street (The Upper East Side, Upper West Side, Lenox Hill, Carnegie Hill, Yorkville, etc.)

- Upper Manhattan-the area above 96th Street (Inwood, Harlem, Washington Heights, Fort George, Morningside Heights, etc.)

- Downtown Manhattan-the area below 14th Street (NoHo, East Village, West Village, Lower East Side, Alphabet City, Greenwich Village, Nolita, SoHo, etc.)

- Between Downtown and Midtown- (Kips Bay, Gramercy Park, Chelsea, Flatiron District, Union Square, Waterside Plaza, Stuyvesant Town, etc.)

- Lower Manhattan-the area below Chambers Street. (TriBeCa, Financial District, Battery Park City, Chinatown, Little Italy, etc.)

- Midtown Manhattan-the area between 34th Street and 59th Street (Midtown, Columbus Circle, Sutton Place, Rockefeller Center, Diamond District, Turtle Bay, Madison Square, Hell's Kitchen, Times Square, Herald Square, Murray Hill, Garment District, etc.)

- The West Side refers to the area west of Fifth Avenue, while the East Side refers to the area east of Fifth Avenue. In the cases of the Upper

East Side and the Upper West Side, the two areas are split by Central Park.

Tricks for Street Orientation: Walk Like a True New Yorker!

Here are some useful memory tricks that are easy to remember and might help you get your bearings in NYC.

- Although the island of Manhattan is actually tilted toward the northeast, everyone here uses north/south, or uptown/downtown.

- Traffic on 1st Ave, 3rd Ave, and Amsterdam Ave goes north, aka uptown. You can remember this by picturing the number 1 as a rocket (it goes up), the number 3 as two balloons (they go up), and the letter "A" as the head of an arrow pointing up.

- Traffic on 2nd Ave, 5th Ave, and Columbus Ave goes south, or as New Yorkers call it, "downtown". You can remember this by thinking of the numbers 2 and 5 as being s-shaped (for "south"), and the word "Columbus" as the country Columbia, which is south of NYC.

- Streets run east/west. Even streets run east, which you can remember by thinking of how "even" and "east" start with the same letter, while odd streets run the opposite way (west)

- Street addresses use "west" or "east" depending on which side of Fifth Avenue you're on—for example, 157 E 68th Street and 157 W 68th Street. You know you're not a local when...you mistake is to walk the wrong direction along a street because you're looking for the address on the wrong side of Fifth Avenue

- Houston Street is pronounced "HOWston" not "HOOUSTON"

- When giving directions in a cab, make sure to say the street first and then the avenue. Example: "I need to go to 71st and 2nd please. AND STEP ON IT!"

Each of Manhattan's neighborhoods pack diversity and culture into each area, which makes it hard to choose which neighborhoods to travel to, especially if your travel is limited. Most of the iconic New York areas and skyscrapers such as the Empire State Building, Chrysler Building, the United Nations and Times Square are found in the heart of the Big Apple: Midtown Manhattan. The Financial District holds major corporate hubs such as the Freedom Tower, the World Trade Center Memorial, as well as many international corporations. Cultural areas mostly speak for themselves in their name. From Chinatown to Little Italy to Little Korea you can find some of the world's best ethnic cuisine at the drop of a hat.

Transportation is not only accessible but also easy to understand throughout Manhattan and its boroughs. Whether by bus or subway, locals commute on publish transportation. Although they may moan and groan about delays or subway construction, it's much more affordable than a taxicab, and can take you home sometimes in the same amount of time. Everywhere in Manhattan and the other boroughs are connected through one line or another. Chapter five of this guide provides detailed information on how to effectively use New York City's public transportation like a pro.

Understanding Manhattan's Neighborhoods

Manhattan's neighborhoods are as unique as their residents. Depending on the neighborhood, you can find that shopping, museums, and even culture vary depending on the location. When you're looking at where to go, where to stay, or where to eat, we've compiled a few noteworthy destinations for each neighborhood!

Upper West Side

The iconic Upper West Side is known for its "old money" roots and high end suits. From baby strollers to dog walkers, the Upper West Side is indeed the most family oriented of the more popular Manhattan neighborhoods. Traditional brownstone buildings line the streets with picturesque views. Many of the most expensive retail shopping is available in this area, along with quiet tree strewn streets and local bakeries. Keep an eye out for celebrities, as many prefer this posh and quiet neighborhood. The Lincoln Center for the Arts, prestigious Columbus Circle, and satellite classrooms to the prestigious Fordham University and Columbia University can be found in the Upper West Side.

Upper East Side

The Upper East Side is one of the more quiet neighborhoods of New York. Located along the east side of famed Central Park, it extends from 59th Street to 96th street. Important museums run along the Upper East Side's section of Fifth Avenue, which is nicknamed the "Museum Mile". This "mile" includes the Metropolitan Museum of Art (www.metmuseum.org/), the Jewish Museum of New York (www.thejewishmuseum.org), The Frick Collection (www.frick.org), as well as the Guggenheim Museum (www.guggenheim.org), among others. Although the subways run along Lexington Avenue, stroll down to 2nd Avenue, where an array of local known restaurants and pubs are found along the street.

Midtown

If looking for New York City's renowned bright lights and city hustle, then head to Midtown. This small neighborhood is not to be judged by size, as its streets are home to some of the most well known buildings such as Chrysler Building, Grand Central, and the Empire State Building, and the iconic Bryant Park. Be sure to look at the New Year's Eve Ball and the bright billboards in Times Square.

Hell's Kitchen

Due to the large corporations and tourist attractions like Times Square, you will find your most expensive options for dining and nightlife in Midtown. Popular chains and retail stores reside closer to Times Square. If you're traveling on a budget or looking for local cuisine, walk west to 9th Avenue in Midtown to the Hell's Kitchen neighborhood. Hell's Kitchen, also known as Clinton or the Midtown West neighborhood, is located between 34th to 59th street, between Eighth Avenue and the Hudson River. "Restaurant Row" is located between 8th and 9th Avenue in Hell's Kitchen.

Lower East Side

The Lower East Side is seen as one of the "trendier" areas of New York. It consists of shorter buildings, street graffiti, street vendors, and laid-back vibe are a far cry from looking like the tall cityscape of Midtown. Whether in the mood for a quick bite at the famous Katz's Deli (katzsdelicatessen.com), or strolling the streets to view the street art, the LES filled with buzzing restaurants and bars.

East Village

If you're looking for something a little off the beaten path, the East Village is for you. Don't be weary of the graffiti signed walls and flannel wearing hipsters. Instead, bask in the freedom of art. The East Village is known for its vibrant history in the arts and nightlife. Their kitschy restaurants are unusual and delicious; so don't be afraid to go right in! Some of the best coffee houses are in the East Village such as the East Village Coffee Lounge.

SoHo

SoHo is known for its eclectic shopping, art galleries, and restaurants. The traditional cobblestone streets of New York's past offer landmark cast iron buildings, which hold some of the most unique and pricier shopping in the world. Whether looking for local boutiques, chain retail stores, or high-end items, SoHo has every shop you could want.

Brooklyn-Williamsburg

The rapidly growing Brooklyn area of Williamsburg has a lot to offer if you're willing to take the journey. The easiest access is by subway. The redefined Williamsburg area will likely surprise you, as its recycled and renovated industrial buildings hold new apartment buildings and local businesses.

Bedford Avenue, the longest street in Brooklyn, is known for its versatile nightlife and gorgeous brownstone buildings.

Brooklyn-DUMBO

DUMBO stands for Down Under Manhattan Bridge Overpass, and is one of Brooklyn's fastest growing neighborhoods. From exclusive art galleries to Brooklyn Bridge State Park, DUMBO is becoming a trendy area for startups and boutiques. The East River Ferry stops at the Brooklyn Bridge Park, and allows scenic views of the skyline as well as Brooklyn and Queens.

Queens-Astoria

Astoria is 15 minutes or less from Midtown Manhattan by subway or cab. The N and W subways lines run through the heart of the vibrant neighborhood, above 31st Street. This area is not known for its heavy nightlife, but rather its authentic restaurants and corner bars. From a bohemian beer garden to breathtaking views of the skyline, Queens is not to be forgotten on your stop.

Queens-Long Island City

Many become confused between Long Island and Long Island City. Long Island City is currently under a dramatic renovation and revitalization. Luxury apartments with amazing views of the skylines are rising every day, and there is a reason for it. Long Island City's bars and restaurant nightlife is upping their game. With only one stop on the subway from Manhattan, it's easy to get to and worth the trip. From Skinny's Cantina mouthwatering margaritas to the relaxed atmosphere of the Alewife Pub, Long Island City offers something for anyone's taste.

Chapter 2
Things You Must Absolutely Do and See In New York

As we've said before, New York is what you make of it. From the thousands of restaurants, dozens of original Broadway shows, to the art and nightlife scenes, New York City is a mecca for anything you can dream of. As any New Yorker will tell you, there's no way to see all the highlights of this vast, complex city in just one visit. That's part of the thrill of visiting the Big Apple—there's always something new to discover. From iconic landmarks to local favorites these essentials must be at the top of your list.

The "City That Never Sleeps" is a fast paced, hustling, metropolitan island filled with dreams and go-getters. Countless movies, television shows, and other forms of media place their settings in New York due to its limitless boundaries and interesting characters. As a cultural melting pot, many true "New Yorkers" are actually not be originally from New York. Those that have wanted to follow the New York dream have moved to fulfill their goals. In return, they have developed certain characteristics/preferences that they learn and evolve to in New York will make them locals. We've compiled a list of ways you not only can spot a New Yorker in New York City, but also how you can spot them outside of their habitat.

Ways to Spot a true New Yorker in New York City (so you know how to act like one)

- **A New Yorker is always running/rushing to get places.**

Whether it's a bus, subway train, or cab, a local New Yorker is always on the go. They need to be somewhere and they are rushing, because time is money in New York. While "out of towners" or tourists are taking a minute to absorb their surroundings or understand their location and how to get to their next destination, New Yorkers have places to be and people to see. If you are the unfortunate person to block a New Yorker from their way, beware to be told to move!

- **2. You can't find a New Yorker in Times Square.**

Further continuing our first point, a New Yorker will find the quickest route to get to where they need to be. With that, they wouldn't be caught in extremely populated/touristy areas such as Washington Square, Times Square, or Union Square, unless they are showing family and friends around the city.

- **A New Yorker is not stopping in the middle of the streets to take a picture**

If they're taking a minute to stop and take a picture of a skyscraper, they aren't a "true New Yorker". Yes, the skyscrapers are amazing. However, we see them day in and out, and the places New Yorkers need to be are more important than "stopping to smell the roses".

- **They're not looking at you. They're looking down, past you, or at their phones.**

A New Yorker is too busy to be bothered with simple pleasantries. With over 8 million people living in New York City, they don't need to worry about being polite. They are doing five things at once; making sure to use their time wisely.

- **When they walk by a celebrity, they don't freak out.**

Many celebrities live in New York City. A true New Yorker views them as another person, just trying to do their job and live in the city. While a tourist may get excited and ask for a photo with said celebrity, a local is too cool for that.

- **Most of their wardrobe is black.**

New Yorkers like simple. Black is simple, chic, and always in style.   A New Yorker won't wear loud prints, colors, or patterns. They'll stick with what's classic and easy to wear.

- **They'll be the ones yelling at a New York Bar**

Whether they are a Giants/Yankees or a Jets/Mets fan, a New York fan is a diehard fan. Just because they may have moved outside of New York, doesn't mean they'll stop rooting for them.   With all the transplants across the United States, it's easy to assume there will be a New York bar somewhere and it will be filled with proud New Yorkers.

- **They'll have their headphones on.**

New Yorkers spend countless hours on public transportation in the city. It doesn't matter if they are in New York or another city, as this habit will transfer with them. It's more important to be focusing in on their work/transportation, then casual chitchat.

- **They know the latest websites/apps for finding restaurants/modern conveniences.**

If a New Yorker doesn't know about the latest restaurant like they would in their normal comfort zone of Manhattan, they know to use Yelp or another app to find out where to go. If they need a cab, they know not to wait outside or call a cab company, but to Uber. If they want to get laundry done, buy groceries, or pick up their medication, they know to order it online. New Yorkers know how to do many things at once. One way to do this is by knowing the latest and greatest apps or websites to make life easier.

- **They can only speak badly about New York.**

If a New Yorker moves away from the city, they'll talk about New York. Whether it's the hustle, the trash, the smells, or the transportation, they'll give a reason why they moved. However, don't fall into this trap and chime in. In reality, a true New Yorker has a love/hate relationship with the city. They'll complain about it and talk about what they went through while living there as if it was a war story. A true New Yorker will ultimately know it's like no other, will always remain loyal to it, and their heart will ache when they move away from it.

New York Highlights

Get a taste of the city with top highlights, ranging from historical to mouthwatering, famous, and the unusual.

Get Out In the Concrete Jungle and EXPLORE! Highlights that involve you getting outside, getting moving, and are a MUST DO!

- **Central Park:** One of the most famous and iconic parks in the world, Central Park's 343-acre oasis is a haven for bikers, runners, locals, and tourists. Hundreds of movies have been filmed in this park for a reason, and it's the top of our "To Do" list. The best part? The admission is free! Walk around the Jackie O'Nassis' Reservoir, watch a youth baseball game, grab a pretzel from a vendor, or take a ride on Central Park's Friedsam Memorial Carousel. Boat rentals are available at the Boathouse, along with wine and a restaurant. Head to the West Side of the park to pay homage to Strawberry Fields; a tribute to the late John Lennon. If you're feeling in the need for a run, take one of the paths through the Upper West Side's Columbia Hills for a work out that will be sure to leave you out of breath. Other attractions include Belvedere Castle, the Sheep Meadow, the Great Lawn, and the Central Park Zoo.

- **The High Line:** In 1934, the city of New York built a high-line railway to cut back on the exorbitant number of accidents pedestrians were having with the street-level trains. The new technology of the underground rail diminished railway traffic, and later it was decommissioned. From the water, this park can be viewed in Manhattan's Chelsea/West Side as an overgrown suspending track.

New Yorkers love to walk along the 1.45-mile-long High Line, an elevated park above the streets of Manhattan. This unique park stretches from Gansevoort Street in the Meatpacking District through Chelsea, and up to West 34th street on a previously derelict, elevated railway track. Resurrected with an incredible maze of gardens (showcasing 300 species of plants), pathways, and water features, it offers amazing views of both the Hudson River and the city. The High Line takes you past the Chelsea Market, the popular Standard Hotel, and a western view of the Empire State Building.

- **The Statue of Liberty:** Whether looking from Brooklyn Bridge, Battery Park, or onboard the Staten Island Ferry, you cannot go to New York City without seeing the Statue of Liberty. At a staggering 151 feet tall, the Statue of Liberty is one of the most iconic statues today.

- **The Elevated Acre Park:** Similar to the West Side's High Line, this park offers amazing views of the Brooklyn Bridge, Hudson River, and the iconic Statue of Liberty. This one-acre space offers area for locals to walk, lay out in the sun, or even mini golf. From the water, view the small park in the Financial District and see the obscure passage of grassy field caught between two skyscrapers

- **Grand Central Terminal:** Packed with history as well as angry commuting locals, Grand Central Terminal is a New York treasure. This 100-year-old station's impressive main concourse offers breathtaking cathedral-like windows, ornate chandeliers, as well as a Constellation mural on the high ceilings. Head to the Grand Central Concourse, where the food court offers an oyster bar, famous Magnolia's Bakery treats, Shake Shack, and other New York delicacies.

- **Times Square:** A true New Yorker knows not to be caught dead in Times Square during the day, especially when they have places to be or if it's the holiday season. The hustle of Times Square is a nightmare to locals, but that's not to say it's not treasured. As a tourist, it's a cultural hub of the iconic digital billboard bright lights and busy streets that NYC is known for. Although its previous past was quite criminal, excited tourists snapping selfies and sitting on the lighted bleachers above the TKTS booth now overrun it. If you've never traveled to NYC, then Times Square is a must. Bask in the neon lights, listen to the guitar-playing Naked Cowboy, and take a photo with Spiderman or Batman. Head to the M&Ms store for souvenirs, or get in line for discounted Broadway show tickets at the TKTS Discount Ticket Booth (underneath the neon bleachers), watch the ball drop on New Year's Eve or grab a meal along Restaurant Row (West 46th Street, between Eighth and Ninth Avenues).

- **The Brooklyn Bridge:** Admire the skyline as you walk from Manhattan to Brooklyn (we recommend traveling from Brooklyn to Manhattan for truly stellar views) over the iconic Brooklyn Bridge on the pedestrian pathway. Take in the historical architecture of the bridge's high Gothic arches.

- **9/11 Memorial:** When New York City was devastated by terrorist attacks on September 11, 2001, the skyline and Americans would never be the same. Over a decade later, the new Freedom Tower resides as the tallest building in the Western Hemisphere, with a memorial for the World Trade Center's twin towers built next to it. The 9/11 Memorial has cascading reflecting pools on top of where the 110-story buildings once stood with the names of those lost in the attacks. The memorial is emotional yet shows the resilience of the city and the country itself.

- **Corona Park (Flushing Meadows, Queens):** Best known as the location for a little tennis match known as the US Open, Flushing Meadows Corona Park is New York Metropolitan's fourth-largest park. It was the sight of two world fairs and cinematically known for the alien fight scene in *Men In Black.* Other Flushing Meadows–Corona Park attractions include the Queens Botanical Garden, Queens Theater, Queens Zoo, and the New York Hall of Science.

- **New York Public Library:** This library is the second largest in the United States. Its tall historical columns share a block with Bryant Park. Although free, the New York Public Library is truly a gem to the city. Inside lies literature treasures such as Truman Capote's cigar case, Charles Dickens' favorite letter opener, and the original Winnie the Pooh and friends stuffed animals.

- **The Empire State Building:** The view atop the skyscraper's 86th floor observation deck is breathtaking. In preparation of long lines and disgruntled tourists, be weary of weekends. The best time to visit the Empire State Building is between noon and five, where most locals are staying safely in their offices before taking their harried commute. **Insider's Tip:** It's one of the top places to be proposed to in New York City.

The Ultimate "To Do" List for the Stomach-Where to Eat in New York

- **Whether you fold it, roll it, or eat it whole, make sure to grab a slice of Pizza:** No one takes pizza more seriously than New York City. The Italians may have created pizza, but the New Yorkers perfected it. Lombardi's on Spring Street is known for its thin crust, fresh mozzarella, and oven "cracker like" crispness; Patsy's Pizzeria off Third Avenue or in Chelsea is known for its addicting homemade sauce; Artichoke Pizza is known for their creamy spinach-artichoke slice; Sal & Carmine's on Broadway (at 102nd Street) for its cheesy, gooey slice

- **Eataly** is a culinary masterpiece. Located in the Flatiron District (or the Chelsea Neighborhood) Eataly is one part gourmet market and the other part Italian food court. From handmade pasta, seasonal fish, prosciutto, fresh mozzarella, wine, chocolate, pastries, and all the other delicious Italian delicacies, Eataly has you covered.

- **Nothing is more American than a burger, so head to Shake Shack:** This burger joint has blow up since it's opening in 2004. Known for its burgers, fries, shakes, and unique flavors of ice cream, this Danny Meyer Empire is both affordable and worth the long wait in line. Head to the original location in Madison Square Park where it all started.

- **Big Gay Ice Cream** in the East Village is known for their gourmet concoctions. From the "Mermaid" (Vanilla Ice Cream, Key Lime Curd, Whipped Cream, and Crushed Gram Crackers) to their unusual Ginger Curry Milkshake, you'll be sure to try something you've never had before...and leave happy. We guarantee it.
- **Blue Bottle Coffee** may be one of the hippest places in New York City, but don't think it's a fad. Their slow drip iced coffee is strong, delicious, and will keep you going throughout the day.

Noteworthy Museums

- **The Metropolitan Museum of Art**: Ranking among the world's best art museums, this Upper East Side Museum houses everything from Medieval and Expressionist masterpieces to an entire Egyptian temple. Yes, you've heard right. The Greek and Roman sculptures, African and Oceania exhibits, and Asian Wing are also pretty amazing. If you wake up and it's raining, head to the Met (open seven days a week) and wander. Bonus: The Museum's website offers itineraries and maps to make sure you hit areas that peak your interest

- **Solomon R. Guggenheim Museum**-Designed by Frank Lloyd Wright and inspired by a simple conch shell, the Guggenheim Museum is another Upper East Side gem. One of the most iconic buildings of the mid-20th century, the Museum alone is worth visiting too. The artwork on the inside is the added bonus.

- **City Reliquary-**This *Williamsburg, Brooklyn* is definitely for those who love the unusual. Originally a first-floor apartment, then turned "oddities" shop, and now just a haven for the weird, tourists and locals alike travel to this Metropolitan Avenue museum to see the unconventional. From subway paint chips to city signs to an exhibit on pennies flattened from the pressure of city traffic, their constantly rotating exhibits will amuse you.

- **Museum of Sex-**The Flatiron District's museum of sex includes oddities definitely not for the refined. Dedicated to tart a museum dedicated to "the history, evolution and cultural significance of human sexuality" this museum features medieval sex toys to sex chairs to the effects of pinup girls in the 50s.

- **Lincoln Center for the Performing Arts:** Offering thousands of performances ranging from traditional to unique each year, Lincoln Center has established itself as a mecca for New York City's performing arts scene. The Upper West Side complex is home to 11 organizations, which includes the Metropolitan Opera, the New York

City Ballet, as well as Mercedes Benz Fashion Week. Its extensive list of organizations offers many outdoors concerts, plays and film screenings throughout summer months.

- **St. Patrick's Cathedral:** The Neo-Gothic-style Roman Catholic Church is located in Midtown Manhattan along Fifth Avenue. The Cathedral takes up an entire block, and historically sticks out among the hustle of surrounding retail stores.

Activities Galore!

- **Bronx Zoo:** The 265 acre Zoo is the largest urban wildlife preserve in the United States. Its home to more than 5,000 animals, with over 600 species. Daily attractions include feeding the penguins and sea lions, a Bug Carousel, among other seasonal activities. Like many of the museums in New York City, the Zoo offers the option to "pay what you wish" every Wednesday.

- **Yankee Stadium:** The original Yankee Stadium was built in 1923 and was known as "The House That Ruth Built," The new Yankee Stadium opened in 2009, and the team capped the venue's inaugural season with its 27th World Series title. This iconic stadium is a must-see for any baseball fan. Visitors have the option to take a guided tour, which allows stops at the batting cage area, dugout, and Monument Park. The New York Yankees Museum also resides in the Stadium, which offers pieces of the old stadium and other memorable treasures.

Infamous Photo Opportunities

- Stand directly in front of Time's Square with the billboards and lights behind you

- Take a photo while eating a hot dog or bag of peanuts at Yankee Stadium

- Sit on the iconic steps of the Metropolitan Museum of Art

- Photos walking the Brooklyn Bridge with the Skyline behind

- Ice Skating at Bryant Park

- Taking an angry cab selfie

- Recreating *Home Alone* Kevin McAllister's scared face in front of the Plaza Hotel

- Go ice skating (weather permitting) in famous Rockefeller Center

- Sit on the steps of the Metropolitan Museum of Art and pose like the girls in *Gossip Girl*

The "I Can't Believe I Just Did That" New York Moment

- Take the Staten Island Ferry and view the Statue of Liberty and Historical Ellis Island. Did we mention there's a bar on the ferry?

- Take the hour-long subway ride to Coney Island and get a famous Nathan's hotdog while strolling along the boardwalk.

- Walk downstairs to the Food Court of Grand Central. In the entryway before the famous Oyster Bar, whisper into the columned arches while someone else listens directly diagonally. You'll be surprised what you hear!

- Go to Mehanata Bar in the Lower East Side, dress in the bartender's choice of fur jacket, and try to drink as many shots as you can in the Ice Bar.

- Dance the night away in the prestigious Boom Boom Room at the Standard Hotel with floor to ceiling views of the Hudson River and New York Skyline

- Take an adventure to the underground Brooklyn Night Bazaar in Williamsburg, where you can eat from favorite local food trucks, drink cocktails, play pick up soccer, or browse the vendors. http://bkbazaar.com/

- Ride the subway (6) line to the end of the stop and do not get off at Brooklyn Bridge. As the train loops around, it passes the incredible abandoned and lit City Hall Subway Stop

- Go to the top of the Empire State Building

Chapter 3
Planning Your Trip Ahead (Tips & New York Itinerary

When planning a trip to New York City, it should be 50 percent planned and 50 percent completely unplanned. With so many restaurants, shops, bakeries, coffeehouses, and tourism attractions, it would be unfair to the city itself to plan every single minute. Make sure to take time to fully wing it and just walk the streets. Sit in a park and people watch. You'll be glad in the fast paced world of New York that you took a minute to take it all in!

First, Get it Together and Get Orientated

Do as the New Yorkers do: check out upcoming free events/concerts on http://livingfreenyc.com/ and check in with the up-to-date Web site www.nycitysearch.com . The Groupon App offers great local deals on activities, restaurants, and tourist excursions (groupon.com)

Depending on where you want to go, how long you're staying, and what you want to see, think about buying a nine-day **New York CityPass** www.citypass.com; available online or at the six attractions covered; (adults $53, children under 17 $41),. The CityPass is for those who want to move on a "New York Minute". It takes you to the head of the line and takes half off the price of admission at six of the city's most popular stops, including the Empire State Building and the American Museum of Natural History. Upon arrival in town, take advantage of the **New York's Official Visitor Information Center** (810 Seventh Ave., at 52nd St.) to chat with tour guides, gather brochures, find more local discounts, and which way to your hotel.

Once you have your itinerary set, make your way to a park or your hotel for free Wi-Fi. Download the Uber, Roadify, and Yelp apps to find out your information like a true New Yorker.

- **Uber**-If you don't feel like waiting for a cab or taking the subway, you can schedule a ride with your GPS from where you are. The Uber may be slightly pricier than a cab, but it's worth it especially if you're in a time crunch or are in rush hour.

- **Roadify**-Roadify is one of the best transportation apps around. It tells you which subway lines or buses you need to take, as well as gives you pricing estimates for your cab ride. If there are delays, construction on the lines, or a traffic jam, it will tell you. Rest easy and just follow the instructions. If you're caught without a subway map, Roadify has all the MTA maps and guides available on there and are easy to download.

- **Yelp-**When browsing for restaurants, it's best to take the suggestions of locals. Instead of asking, why not use an app to just show you the ratings of the best restaurants in the shortest distance? Yelp is one of the most commonly used apps in New York and it's free!

- **Tweat.It-**New York City is known as a major hub for food trucks. From Gorilla Cheese's Gourmet Grilled Cheeses to the Taco Truck to grabbing a waffle kabob from Waffels and Dinges, the food truck world is your oyster. However, with limited time in the city, how do you know where to go and get the best grub? By using the Tweat.it app, you can locate food trucks that are close by or favorites in your search bar. Much like yelp, you can search different food options to get the best truck for your palette. Try the Cupcake Truck.

http://tweat.it/mobile

Other Important Tips:

- Try to see different sides of New York City. Whether at the top of the Empire State Building, at the Top of the Rock, on a ferry, or high above the skyline in a helicopter, it's worth getting new perspective.

- Frank Sinatra once sang in *New York, New York* that "If you can make it here, you can make it anywhere". He wasn't wrong! New York is an overwhelming place. If you're not used to walking around as much, plan for a nap. If you get dizzy or hungry, make sure to either bring a snack with you or grab something. There's a coffee shop on every corner. If you're overwhelmed by the fast pace, find a bench, breath and soak it all in.

- While planning your trips, be sure to tack on an hour to your commute. With public transportation stops, walking to and from the subway/bus stop, as well as potentially getting lost, it's more likely to take more time than less.

- Avoid those trying to offer you "free comedy tickets". They can be found in popular areas such as Times Square, Union Square, or around Bryant Park. These tickets always come with a price, and usually that means admission to the club and a minimum of two free drinks.

- Never show your wallet or money in public. Always be careful to conceal it. No matter how safe the area, New York City is still a big city and with more population comes more crime. Think smart and you'll be fine!

New York Through the Seasons: When to Go and What to Expect

New York offers the beautiful four seasons offered by the northern part of the United States. However, some times the weather isn't as ideal for tourists (especially if you aren't used to it). Manhattan resides between two rivers (the East River and the Hudson River). Because of this and its proximity to the Atlantic Ocean, the temperatures tend to drop at night and stay extra chilly during the winters.

New York City can be hot, humid, sunny, cold, rainy, sticky, frigid, or beautiful...and New Yorkers accept all of it with stride (and a glare). Here are the seasonal expectations so you know what to pack and plan for!

- **Winter (October to late February):** Outside of Christmas and New Year, this is the quietest time to visit. From October to the New Year, New York City is the busiest and the most expensive because of the Holiday Season. There is something magical about a light snow After the holidays, many are tired of partying, celebrating, gifting, and traveling, so that also means that New York is the cheapest during this time. From hotels to restaurant deals to tourist packages, do your research and plan ahead to ensure a good rate. However, the downside is the limited daylight, the frigid temperatures and icy sidewalks. Invest in a good pair of snow boots, mittens, a puffer coat, and you'll fit right in with the other disgruntled and cold New Yorkers.

- **Spring (March to early May):** Spring is one of the shortest seasons in New York, but it's one of the most beautiful. As the days become longer and flowers and trees start to bloom, the New York Attitude tends to thaw out (just a little). If you plan your trip around this time, be sure to head to the Upper West or Upper East Side and view the gorgeous bright pink cherry blossoms blooming on the trees. Be prepared to bring a medium weight jacket and long pants due to cooler mornings and dropping temperatures when the sun goes down.

- **Summer (Middle May to late August):** Because school is out, summer in New York City is peak season and swarming with crowds just as crowded as the holiday season. Surprisingly, although prices may soar, July 4th Weekend is one of the quietest in the city as many locals flee the high temperatures for the beach or a body of water. New York City on a summer day can be quite hot and humid, so be prepared to wear less. Although it is hot, if you plan on walking a lot be prepared to wear close-toed shoes to not get stepped on in the busy streets.

  During Memorial Day Weekend, New York City celebrates the popular Fleet Week, a week in which active military ships recently deployed in overseas operations dock for celebrations for one week. Be prepared for busy streets filled with uniformed men, and the single ladies that flock not too far behind.

- **Autumn (September to October):** As schools become back in session, the crowds for popular tourist sites tend to die down. The days are still warm, the weather is still pleasant, and the humidity has waned down. Fall is the best time to visit New York City, as the leaves are changing and a cooler breeze keeps the subway rides from being hot and sticky. In early November, the New York City Marathon is one of the best and notable races to watch, as the city shuts down and celebrates the runners who reached this feat.

Chapter 4
Where to Sleep (Hotels, Hostels, Tips, & More)

Real estate is extremely expensive in New York City. Most locals spend 50% of their salaries on rent. Although you're not in the market for purchasing, you should take into consideration that if land and property is expensive, the rent or hotel will be expensive. The closer the hotel/hostel is from major attractions, the pricier it will become. Below, you'll find insider tips on where to look, some great hotel listings to consider for any budget, and where else to look to suit your travel needs.

This guide only lists well-recommended accommodations. Be sure to do your research and take the tips into consideration before purchasing.

Proximity to the Subway

Most hotels will advertise that they are in close proximity to bars, shops, and attractions. The lower the price, the lesser the truth behind that statement. The most important things a tourist should look at is the close proximity to where they want to go, the ratings and comments from past travelers, and the actual distance from public transit. Even the prestigious Waldorf Astoria hotel had a case of bed bugs! Read the reviews and call the hotel for any questions before you book. You can purchase a stay at a beautiful water's edge hotel, but if you don't want to walk four long avenues in the frigid cold when you're planning a trip in the winter, you may want to rethink location.

You Don't Have to Spend $400+ A Night to Find a Great Hotel

Thanks to the subway systems and other public transport, you don't need to stay in the heart of Midtown Manhattan. Staying somewhere off the beaten track is exciting and always makes for a good story! As we've said before, the farther away you move from popular tourist attractions (let's say Times Square), the cheaper the price will be. The further you get to the water, the cheaper the price will be (because you have to walk further to transportation). If you're planning to have an active nightlife and don't want to walk (or want to wear a pair of killer heels) keep in mind that taxicabs can add up and add up quick. If you're willing to compensate a less expensive hotel for more money in cab rides, then by all means-the hotel options are YOUR Oyster!

Take Advantage of Hotel Deals

From Travelzoo to Hotwire to Groupon to Kayak, there are enough travel sites to give you whiplash. When looking at hotels, do your research and find the best deal. Websites such as Priceline.com offer refunds if you find a cheaper price. Hotwire offer's "Hotel Roulette" which means you pay the price, find the area, and they'll match you with a hotel of that value or greater. Do your research and you'll be happy to save the extra $$$

Budget, Budget, Budget

Yes, it may be your vacation, but budgeting cannot hurt. When people think of New York City, they think of the posh, SoHo loft apartments, sprawling from one end of the block to the next with amazing skyline views. Let's be realistic. Most locals don't live like that, and most hotels don't have rooms like those unless you're willing to spend the big bucks. Lower your expectations and plan your budget. If you don't have a view, don't sweat it! Many hotels offer rooftop bars so you can get those sprawling views of the city. Save a little and you'll be glad when you did when you get your dinner bill.

Accommodation Options and Listings

As a major financial, commerce, technology, and fashion capital, New York City stays up to date and on trend with accommodations. Hotels and hostels compete with each other in the "dog eat dog" environment, so your options will be distinctly different and hard to choose. Rather than being stuck with hundreds of options, and no idea where to go in a foreign city, this guidebook offers you a variety of accommodations for any preference. From "Dorm-like" hostels to 5 star hotels, we give you a little piece of everything. If you're planning on booking a trip in the Summer (June to August) or Holiday (December to January) months, expect prices to go up due to inflation and popularity.

Hostels

In the 1970s, 1980s, and even early 1990s, New York City had a lot of shady areas. Nowadays, New Yorkers have seen a vast improvement in hotels, hostels, and other accommodations. Hostels are great traveling options for the traveler on a budget. Hostels continue to be the most affordable lodging option in the city, and with the constant competition of reasonable hotels and apartment sharing websites; they've started to up their game with modern amenities such as free Wi-Fi. If you don't mind sharing a room with a stranger (or new friend, depending on how you look at it) hostels can be a great and affordable option. Many hostels also offer locker and safe options so that you won't have to worry about your belongings when you're out on the town.

- **Bowery's Whitehouse** – Walking distance from NYU, Greenwich Village, the Lower East Side, and Soho, this hostel is accommodating and great for those who live for the nightlife. They offer laundry on premises, as well as complimentary linens and towels. www.whitehousehotelofny.com

- **Chelsea International Hostel** –located in historic Chelsea, this hostel is in a safe and great location in between the vibrant nightlife of Greenwich Village and Hell's Kitchen, offers airport shuttle, and is reasonably priced. This hostel is extremely close to the Chelsea location of the Meatball Shop, which will leave you wanting to be rolled home and grateful you won't have to walk far. www.chelseahostel.com

- **Williamsburg Hostel-** If you're hitting up the trendy bars of Williamsburg, Brooklyn, this hostel resides directly on one of the most popular streets: Bedford Avenue. You're only a stone's throw away from local favorites such as Turkey's Nest and the Black Swan. Rates start at $69 a night and can only be booked through third party booking sites such as Hotels.com.

- **The Jane Hotel-**With rates as low as $79 a night, this West Village hostel is a gem. Fun fact, this hotel used to be a boarding haven for sailors and once held survivors of the *Titanic.* After a lengthy renovation, this hotel has been updated to include helpful travel technology such as free Wi-Fi and Ipod docks. *thejanenyc.com.*

- **HI New York-**HI (Hosteling International)'s New York location is their biggest hostel in North America. Holding a whopping 672 rooms, this Upper West hostel starts at an unbelievable $44 a night. It may be an extra few minutes on the subway, but it's worth the price! *hinewyork.org*

- **Zip 112-**Another Bedford Street hostel makes the list because what this Williamsburg location lacks in size it makes up in location and amenities. Linens and towels are provided at time of check in. It's fifth floor walk up, but it's worth the sore muscles for the saved cab fares. *zip112.com*

- **The Pod Hotel-**If traveling in a duo or pairs, this hotel is a steal. The hostel accommodates in bunk pods styling, with pods at $169 per pair. Located in the Midtown East area of Turtle Bay, this hostel is close to local restaurants, pubs, and nightlife. Head to famed Turtle Bay Bar & Grille to see New York City's "best hookup bar". *thepodhotel.com.*

- **International Student Center-** This "dorm like" hostel is centrally located in Manhattan on the Upper West Side, in a safe residential area next to the beautiful Central Park. Subway and buses are easily accessible, and it's location of 88th streets makes it close to local restaurants and bars. http://www.hostels.com/hostels/new-york/international-student-center/4547?p=10#propertyAnchor=p4547

Good Value Hotels

From international hotel chains to shabby chic styled hotels, New York has it all. If you're not willing to pay the luxury prices of the hotels found off Park Avenue, there are many other options that give you the best "bang for your buck". High density populated areas such as Europe and bigger cities such as Manhattan offer a lot less space for a higher rate. When looking for hotels, keep your mind open to possibilities of smaller spaces. New York City offers plenty of boutique hotels located in popular areas. They might not be as popular as a chain hotel, but that doesn't mean they don't know what they're doing! What they lack in outreach, they gain in service. Check out reviews on websites such as Yelp.com or Travelocity.com for a visitor's insight to the hotel itself.

If you're looking for something more personal than a hostel, these value hotels offer a little more space and added comfort...not to mention your own bathroom.

- **Hotel Deauville, Gramercy Park:** Historic Gramercy Park is a great hotel choice not just for location but if you want to hideaway from the busy higher trafficked streets. The rooms are shabby chic styled, and at an affordable $139+ a night option, they're hard to beat. *www.hoteldeauville.com*

- **Best Western Bowery Hanbee Hotel-**Located in eccentric Chinatown, this hotel chain branch is easy walking distance from the neighborhoods of Soho, Little Italy, the East Village and Lower East Side *www.bw-boweryhanbeehotel.com*

- **The Jane-**The Jane's big brothers (downtown favorites the Bowery Hotel and the Maritime) all fall into the same romance esthetic created by designer Sean MacPherson. However, The Jane is one of Greenwich Village's boutique hotels that offers romance in the form of location. The rooms are small, the bathrooms are shared and coed, but the entrance of The Jane puts you in the whimsical winding streets of historic Greenwich Village. Filled with restaurants, hidden bars, and speakeasies, Greenwich Village gives you lively nightlife steps away from the hotel.

- **The Library Hotel-**This chic boutique hotel offers warm and inviting rooms, continental breakfast, competitive rates, and walking distance from major attractions in Midtown Manhattan. For the avid reader, the Library Hotel boasts over 6000 hand-selected books organized by the Dewey Decimal System. This hotel has been noted to have the friendliest and most informative staff. Don't be afraid to ask questions! http://www.libraryhotel.com

- **Hotel Elysee-**If the Midtown Manhattan location and noteworthy and prestigious cocktail bar underneath the hotel don't sell you, then the prices should. Feel like you're paying a kidney for the room with its luxurious 1920s styled décor and popular jazz band downstairs that plays many times a week. http://www.elyseehotel.com/

- **The Iroquois-**Surrounded by Ivy League clubs such as the Harvard and Yale Club, the prestigious Iroquois Hotel is a great Midtown Manhattan option in a central location and value for your money. **http://www.iroquoisny.com/?chebs=tabl-iroquois**

- **Nu Hotel-**This Brooklyn boutique hotel takes modern to the next level. Airy, loft-style rooms have free WiFi, desks, minibars, 42-inch TVs and cork floors. Some suites even offer hammocks to relax in from a long day of exploring. http://nuhotelbrooklyn.com

- **Yotel-570 Tenth Avenue** Yotel is a unique experience in its own. Inspired by Japanese hotels, this futuristic concept offers smaller rooms, where no space is left unused. Yotel offers a Japanese-themed Dohyo that serves meals, and the 7,000 sq ft rooftop terrace with views of the Manhattan skyline is not something to be overlooked. Automated Check In/Out, free Wi-Fi Access, and premium appliances in each room make you feel like you're living in 2514

- **Casablanca Hotel-**147 W. 43rd Street. Located in the heart of Midtown Manhattan, the Casablanca Hotel Times Square is a European-style boutique hotel. Offering Rick's Café, an onsite comfort food mecca, free continental breakfast, complimentary passes to the nearby gym, and Wi-Fi, this hotel is perfect for those that want the most out of their budget. http://www.casablancahotel.com/

Great Hotels to Splurge On

New York has many expensive hotels to splurge on. As a major commerce, financial, and tourist hub, hotels are a dime a dozen. With a city filled with luxury retail shops, impressive 5-star culinary restaurants, and top mixology bars in the world, it's no wonder the hotels have high standards. If you're cutting corners in other areas, why not try out the high life?

- **Four Seasons Hotel** – *Midtown East*: The average hotel room at The Four Seasons (600 square feet) is larger than many New York studio apartments. Located in Midtown East, fourseasons.com

- **Gramercy Park Hotel-**Stunning refurbished wood, illuminating chandeliers, and ornate rugs in the lobby mix old world charm and modern pieces. The Gramercy Park Hotel is worth the splurge http://www.gramercyparkhotel.com

- **The Plaza Hotel-**Whether remembering *Eloise* or *Home Alone*, the iconic Plaza Hotel has kept its luxurious reputation for over a century.

Have tea in the tea room, or enjoy it's Central Park views. www.theplazany.com/

- **Hotel Plaza Athénée-**Located on a quiet Upper East Side block, this hotel is walking distance from prestigious museums such as the MoMA, the Frick Collection, & the Whitney. The hotel offers 24-hour concierge and room service. http://www.plaza-athenee.com/

- **New York Palace-**Walking by this hotel might get you lost in feeling like you're passing a princess castle. It's directly across from St. Patrick's Cathedral in Midtown, a block away from Fifth Avenue shopping, and offers a delicious in hotel restaurant. Make sure to look through your window at night to view the magical lights of the courtyard! http://www.newyorkpalace.com/

- **Wythe Hotel-**Known for its rooftop and master mixologists, the Wythe Hotel is one of Brooklyn's trendiest spots, as well as reasonable hotels.   Check out the floor to ceiling windows that offer a panoramic view of the Manhattan skyline, and take delight in a craft cocktail. Subway tile style bathrooms offer Turkish towels and a cable that hooks to your phone for surround sound systems. The Wythe is walking distance from famed Bedford Avenue, which offers ample vintage boutiques, restaurants, and trendy bars.

Modern Accommodation Options

As technology advances, traveling and personal preferences are constantly changing. People are looking for new and the unusual. Long gone are the days of extreme options on choosing a low budget hostile or a high-end hotel like the Waldorf Hotel.

Renting someone else's apartment: What says "living like a local" more than actually renting a local New Yorker's apartment. The average New Yorker pays over $1300 a month in rent. If you were traveling and weren't using it, you'd want to compensate too! Innovative companies like Air BnB allow you to rent an apartment safely for both the owner and rentee. Find hosts with extra rooms, entire homes, and unique accommodations such as tree houses, rooftop locations, or closet spaces.

Head over to rent an apartment or room at secure sites like www.vrbo.com or www.airbnb.com for renting local apartments or a room.

Sleep on a Couch: For the adventurous type, you can sleep on a couch. Couchsurfing offers the options to stay with locals in someone's home and still experience the city. The website connects a social global network of travelers and volunteers for those who want to view different cities, meet new people, and travel on a budget.

Head to https://www.couchsurfing.com to view New York City options.

Chapter 5
How to Use New York City's Public Transport (Without Getting Lost!)

New York Public Transportation

You'll be surprised by how much time is spent on transportation in New York. Whether walking, taking a cab and stuck in traffic, waiting for the subway/bus, or taking a minute to look at street signs, transportation can be consuming!

New York City Subway

The New York City Subway may seem like a complex system, but once you understand the basics, it's quiet easy to understand in whole. There are 656 miles of subway track that transport commuters to Manhattan, Brooklyn, Queens, Long Island City, the Bronx, and Harlem.
While the word "subway" automatically represents underground trains only, New Yorkers call all municipal rapid transit trains "the subway", even though some of them run above ground. The term also refers only to the trains run by the New York City Transit Authority – it does not include suburban railroads, or the Port Authority's Air Train to the airport and PATH trains to New Jersey. The New York City Subway system extends to four of the five boroughs. It does not extend to Staten Island.

Unlike many international cities, the subway runs 24 hours a day, 7 days a week, 365 days a year. While some stations are sometimes closed for maintenance work or construction, even in those cases there usually shuttle buses provided to provide service to those locations. MTA Apps such as Roadify will be able to tell you about the change in services to avoid the confusion.

The only times the Subway systems have ever closed were during the 2012 Hurricane Sandy storm, where parts of the subways were flooded. Otherwise, the subway never closes.

The fare to ride the subway is presently $2.50 for a single ride.

Depending on your length of stay, there are discounts for multiple ride combinations, and also unlimited fare cards for set periods.) The subway system is made up of a number of different lines that go from one terminal to another in a linear fashion (unlike London, there is no truly circular, looping route.) Where the subway lines intersect in the same or connected stations, you may "transfer" between trains for no cost. Unlike many other cities, it does not matter how far you are riding, or how many times you change trains. If you have paid your fare, you are allowed to ride on that same single fare for as long as you would like (unless you leave the station).

When you enter a subway station, you are in an area that is called the "mezzanine". In the mezzanine can be found the turnstiles, and in most cases the automated subway machines. There are also many large maps of the entire subway system on the wall, as well as the neighborhood map of where you are currently located. The Automated Subway Machines allow you to buy subway ride cards called "MetroCards". While the machine is the easiest to use, if the machine is not working, there is also a subway attendant at the Subway booth directly next to the machines, where you can purchase your tickets.

While all the subways remain in service 24 hours a day, 7 days a week, some less-busy station entrances may be closed at some hours – but the main entrance will be open all the time. You can tell if an entrance is open 24 hours is that there is a green light over it – entrances with red lights are either locked part of the time, or can be accessed only with MetroCards).

MetroCards can be used for either subway service or on the bus service. Depending on the type of MetroCard that you purchased, you can share your card with a friend. You have the option to buy a card with a set dollar amount (which you can increase by adding more money on the card at the Subway Automated Machines), or you can buy a card with unlimited use for a certain period of time. The cards with set monetary values may be used for several riders , while the ones with unlimited rides cannot. Once an unlimited card is used, that card cannot be reused for 18 minutes, to prevent people from passing the card back for reuse by someone else.

Using the MetroCard

Once you have your MetroCard set with your preference of monetary or unlimited value, walk over to the turnstile. There is an electronic device with a slot where you "swipe" your card, at which point the device will give you an electronic message. All turnstiles are "right-handed" devices; swipe in the device on the right side of the turnstile you are entering. The device will give you a message. If it says "go", walk through the turnstile. If it says "swipe again", do so – most first-time users have a tendency to swipe too slowly, and the machine cannot read the card. If it says this message, swipe again.

Finding the Right Subway Train

Once you have entered the turnstile, you continue to the "platform" of the direction that you are going. In most cases, this is further downstairs -- although it may be directly in front of you. Keep in mind that some stations are large complexes, and have more platform areas than one . Look at the signs that show what lines stop there, and also whether that platform is for "uptown" or "downtown" trains. As we have learned, "uptown" means north, while "downtown" means heading south.

The colors of the lines just refer to the streets in midtown Manhattan under which they travel, in order to keep the map from being too confusing. New York City's subway trains are known by their names or numbers, not by their colors. If you become confused, you will confuse a local even more if you are looking for the "orange line". Look for A, or D, or #6, not "blue", "Orange", or "green" trains.

To Take Express or Take Local Trains?

Because of Manhattan's grid like street structure, the subway lines are able to carry trains faster over long distances because of the long avenues. The New York City subway lines have both local trains that stop at every station, and express trains that use a different track and that skip many stations. The express trains only stop at certain major intersecting stations. The express trains will have a filled in circle for every stop they take, while the local trains have a hollow circle, as they take more stops.

For information on New York City's mammoth transit system, including fares and route maps, go to www.mta.nyc.ny.us.

Insider's Tip: Pick up a **$7 Fun Pass**—a one-day MetroCard good for unlimited rides for one person on buses and subways (or, for $24, a seven-day unlimited-ride card; both are also available at subway station vending machines).

The New York City Underground and Overground Subway Map

Taxi-Cabs

You've seen them in television, movies, and all over media. Why not take a cab like a true New Yorker? Oddly enough, most New Yorkers try to take mass transit rather than cabs. However, when you have to get somewhere fast, cabs are efficient and less of a worry. Be aware that most cabs only accommodate four people at most and should be avoided at rush hour (especially if you're trying to get across town during heavy traffic).

Insider's Tip: Stand at the edge of the road with your arm out waiting for a cab. Make sure to lock eyes on the cabs that are available. The only cabs that are available are when their rooftop number is illuminated (it means they do not have someone in the cab) and their off-duty sign is not.

Insider's Tip #2: Black cabs are always more expensive. Try to take a yellow cab if you are looking or you might end up paying 3x the normal fare.

Mobile Transportation Apps

Apps like Uber and Lyft are causing yellow taxicabs to worry. Instead of standing at the edge of the street waving your hand like a maniac, you're able to request a cab. Uber and Lyft both tell you the estimated time of arrival, car to look for, and allow payment through your phone. Beats waiting in the pouring rain for a free taxi!

Ferrys

There are lots of ferry services all around the city, although they go unnoticed by most tourists. Most locals don't even use them unless they're trying to head to Governor's Island for the day or find a way to get to IKEA from the lower tip of Manhattan. (Insider's Tip: it involves a ferry.) Everyone should take a ferry in New York City. If you want to mark it off your bucket list, the Staten Island Ferry is free and offers incredible sights of the Financial District, the Statue of Liberty, Ellis Island, and Staten Island.

The more interesting and probably more useful approach (assuming you're not visiting your Italian in-laws that live on Staten Island), is to try one of the ferries that runs between Manhattan, Queens, and Brooklyn. NY Waterway's East River Ferry will take you from 34th Street in Manhattan to Williamsburg, DUMBO, and Wall Street.

Hudson River Waterway

The NY Waterway runs a water ferry from four stops in Manhattan, as well as stops in Jersey City, Hoboken, Weekhawken, and Edgewater all along the Hudson River. The NY Waterway also provides stops on the East River in Brooklyn and Long Island City. Commuters are allowed to buy tickets through the NY Waterway App on their phones or with cash.

East River Ferry

Starting in 2011, the Ferry offers stops from the Financial District, Midtown East, Brooklyn, Long Island City, and seasonally Governor's Island. Tickets are $4 one way during the week day and $6 one way during the weekend. However, the ferry is a great option to view the city and skyline from the water, as well as see hidden gems such as the abandoned Domino Sugar Factory, Pepsi-Cola sign in Long Island City, and Roosevelt Island. http://www.eastriverferry.com/

Insider Tips: Check out these Hidden Gems!

While many tourists visit New York City to see the top sights, museums, and monuments, many don't realize there are secret wonders right in front of them. Even true New Yorkers miss some of these hidden gems! This concrete jungle may be loud and bright, but there are tons of secrets waiting to be found all in sight…it just depends on how you get there! While many get on the bus or travel by foot, traveling by water offers a different aspect and view of the city. While on your next ferry, look for these views:

• TITANIC MEMORIAL

When the RMS Carpathia delivered the survivors of the world's most infamous ship disaster the Titanic to Pier 54, the Unsinkable Molly Brown insisted on a lighthouse memorial in honor of those who perished at sea. The lighthouse was originally on Manhattan's West Side until 1967, where was moved and now resides on Manhattan's East Side at the South Street Seaport. This eerie sight when viewed from the water takes special meaning.

• Roosevelt Island

Renwick Smallpox Hospital is located between Manhattan and Long Island, on the small strip of land known as Roosevelt Island. The vast immigration from Europe in the 19th to 20th century brought along sickness, and in return a need for this isolated hospital. After the building was left in ruins with the hospital's closing, it was made a landmark in 1972, and is currently under reconstruction. The beautiful Neo-Gothic styled building is prominent on the southern tip of Roosevelt Island, and should not be missed when traveling on water.

• Pepsi Cola Sign

Newly trending Long Island City is home to the Pepsi Cola Sign. Originally on top of the Pepsi Cola Bottling Plant, it's new location in Gantry Plaza overlooks Manhattan and the East River. During sunset or nighttime is best to view this iconic sign.

- The Domino Sugar Factory

The now abandoned Domino Sugar Factory remains as one of New York City's architectural icons, dominates the waterfront of hipster Williamsburg, Brooklyn. With rumors of renovation to the area and removal of the factory, this iconic building is a limited gem and a "must see" before it disappears with other early New York's Industrial buildings.

- The Colegate Clock

Facing the Hudson River, this iconic clock can be found 100 meters next to New Jersey's tallest skyscraper, the Goldman Sachs Tower. The 90-year-old clock faces the Hudson River that survived even after the factory it adorned was demolished in 1988. It's best to view this during sunset or nighttime to see the newly refurbished LED lights.

Planning Your Adventure

As we have talked about in the previous chapters, Manhattan is shaped in a grid-like pattern, with the streets arranging from east to west and the Avenues arranged from North to South. The streets go up in numbers from South to North Manhattan, while the Avenues mix numbers and names from East to West. Whether getting out of the subway or walking down the street, you'll be able to get your bearings better with knowing which way is your direction.

Inside every New York Subway Station, you'll find large local maps of the area. These clear and local maps make finding your destination relatively easy, as long as you follow the streets. By using the Roadify App, you'll be able to have a clearer route, but if you prefer to walk like a New Yorker, follow the grid-like organization of the streets. Attractions are marked and posters are often advertising the destinations on walking routes from the subway stations.

Transport From and To the Airport

Whether traveling from John F. Kennedy, Newark, or LaGuardia airport, buses, subways, and cabs are an option. Cab fares are minimum of $60 per ride, so unless you're traveling with a group of 4, it isn't worth the splurge. It's usually quicker to travel to the center via public transport. Most of all don't be afraid to ask the airport staff! All of the airports offer New York Welcome Centers and will be able to answer most of your questions.

Here are the options for each major airport:

John F. Kennedy International Airport

JFK has many transportation options. From the AirTrain, public subways, and buses, and taxis, public transportation can get you where you need to go. AirTrain JFK provides easy access to both the Long Island Rail Road and MTA's New York City subway and bus system. If NYC is only a pit stop in your journey, JFK is located for regional highway travel and offers car rental opportunities.

LaGuardia Airport

LaGuardia Airport offers a variety of public transportation options to get you into Manhattan. The M60 Bus takes you directly from the airport to 125th street in Manhattan. From there, you can transfer to a subway train to the 1/2/3, 4/5/6, A/C and D **subway trains** (free transfer with MetroCard, otherwise $2.50 additional. The NYC Airporter and Super Shuttler are two bus services outside of Penn Station, Grand Central, or Port Authority that take you directly to the airport and drop you off at your terminals for a cool $13 each way.

Newark Liberty Airport

Like the LaGuardia and JFK Super Shuttler and NYC Airporter, bus services are available to and from the airport from Penn Station, Grand Central, or Port Authority in Manhattan. If heading to the subway trains, use the AirTrain Newark system to connect to a NJ TRANSIT or Amtrak train. Tickets are $5.50.

Chapter 6
Travel Smart, Experience More, and Spend Less

It's a common known fact that New York City is one of the most expensive cities in the world. When traveling, especially with not knowing the conversion off hand, it is hard to understand how much something may cost. If a New Yorker is shaking their head in disbelief, deciding on whether to spend $20 on a cocktail or pay for groceries for the month, then it's easy to understand the shock and horror on a tourist's face.

However, there's a reason we chose to live here and pay the unimaginable prices. New York City is one of the greatest cities in the world, and the experiences are worth the cost. It's a must-see city for any wanderlust traveler, and it can be affordable if you cut the right corners.

How, you ask?
Stick with us.

Sightsee in Midtown Manhattan, but don't spend your whole time there.

Midtown Manhattan is breathtaking. Times Square is a technology phenomenon. The digital billboards, blinking Broadway lights, unbelievable skyscrapers are an absolute must see. Take photos and take plenty. Bask in the sea of tourists, the cramped street walk to the famed square, and take it in. But, know that this is not where the locals reside. Midtown Manhattan is where you'll find those working in finance and tourists. The local delis offer sandwiches for a pricey $15, and if dining in you'll be lucky to spend less than $40 a person. If that deli is mandatory on your list, by all means, grab a bite. However, know that if you walk an Avenue or two either way east or west, you'll be cutting your spending at least 30%. For lunches, my favorite is heading to 2nd Avenue. 2nd Avenue runs along the East Side of Manhattan and is filled with reasonable restaurants, delis, breakfast nooks, and coffee shops. You'll find anything you could ever crave, and you'll be paying almost half the price of Midtown. If you're heading west, Hell's Kitchen offers amazing authentic restaurants significantly cheaper, and within reasonable walking distance.

Save the money for pricier tourist tickets, such as the Empire State Building.

A true New Yorker knows to eat far away from Midtown.

Free Doesn't Mean You're Cheap

Many of New York City's most famous attractions are completely free or offer you the option to "Pay What You Can". Obviously, that rule applies to the honor system; so do pay what you are able to.

Free Attractions:

- Living Free NYC offers a daily, weekly, and monthly list of free attractions going on in New York City http://livingfreenyc.com/

- Museums such as the **Metropolitan Museum of Art** offer the "pay what you can plan". Although they suggest a specific donation, they offer the option to pay what you can in order to entice students and those who would shy away from the usual fees into going. Call ahead or view the websites to make sure there aren't any private.

- **Sony Wonder Technology Lab** allows you to let out your inner sound engineer. Mix sights and sounds or hang out and grab a bite. www.sonywondertechlab.com

- Hang out in **Washington Square Park with the locals and watch serious chess matches**

- Tour the **Federal Reserve Bank** (reservations required) www.ny.frb.org

- Check out New York Artist Walter De Maria's "Earth Room": a SoHo loft filled with 250 cubic yards of dirt www.earthroom.org

- View the world's most comprehensive collection of Native American artifacts at the National Museum of the American Indian www.nmai.si.edu

- During the summer, Bryant Park offers free screenings of classic movies on the big screen on Monday nights. Grab a blanket, some snacks, and enjoy!

- The MoMa offers free Friday night viewings to the public of their art gallery.

Unfortunately for many tourists, free attractions are rarely advertised. Make sure to do your research and save some cash! Visit the **New York's Official Visitor Information Center** (810 Seventh Ave., at 52nd St) to gather brochures, coupons, and talk to a local New Yorker for more advice.

Enjoy the Hotel Breakfast and Find the Supermarkets

If you're balling on a budget, spending money three times a day for meals and snacks can add up. Most New York City hotels offer a continental breakfast, and by taking advantage of this complimentary service, you'll end up cutting corners. For lunch, choose one of the many street lined delis and sandwich shops. From NunPang in Midtown to Lenny's or Brooklyn Bagel, the choices are often reasonably priced and have a large variety to choose from.

Find Coupons and Discounts

Your hotel concierge, the New York Welcome Center, or even websites like Groupon or Yelp offer restaurant and activity discounts. Make sure to take advantage!

Chapter 7
Where to Shop - Crash Guide to New York Best Stores

For those with a passion for fashion and decadent dishes, New York City has one of the most iconic shopping streets.

Travel Essentials

Make sure to wear comfortable shoes as you shop until you drop! The subway has stops along the way, so you won't get lost trying to find transportation.

Essential Experiences

- Window shop along Fifth Avenue and bask in the window displays

- Stop in the iconic Macy's in Herald Square off 34th Street

- Browse SoHo's The Hat Shop Boutique for a truly unique gift.

SoHo:

The cobblestone streets and retail-rich area of SoHo is an intoxicating shopping playground for fashionistas all over. You can shop in Soho for everything from cheap street fashion to upscale designer duds and stylish items for the home. There's even a store for taxidermy. From the fashion favorite Opening Ceremony to small boutiques like Evolution and Kiosk, SoHo's quirky personality is trendy and fun.

Bloomingdale's

This **Upper East Side** (located on Lexington between 59th and 60th Streets) shopping destination is one not to be missed. Besides the countless floors of clothing, shoes, makeup, and accessories, they offer in store food options such as Magnolia Bakery. They have an entire floor dedicated to shoes. Do I have to go on?

Macy's

The original Macy's of the famous widespread retail chain is located in Herald Square at 34th Street is one not to miss. Like Bloomingdale's, it's floors filled with retail goods remind you of Harrod's in London. Macy's also boosts restaurants inside it's store, so you can get your Starbucks caffeine rush when deciding which jacket to buy.

Fifth Avenue:

Fifth Avenue starts all the way up West 142nd Street in Harlem to Washington Square North at Washington Square Park in Greenwich Village. It is filled with some of the most luxurious shopping in the world.

From Kate Spade to Nike Running to H&M, Fifth Avenue has a wide array of stores that you'll want to wander into. Window shop the colorful displays, pop in and out of stores, or get a makeover done at Sephora. Head to the Nike Running Store and run on the treadmills to get custom sneakers suggested specifically for your stride, or go to iconic Tiffany's and stare through the windows like Audrey Hepburn in *Breakfast at Tiffany's*.

Insider's Tip: If heading to New York during the holidays, make sure to walk Fifth Avenue and look at the beautiful and ornate window displays.

Image: World Famous Cartier's Fifth Avenue store decorated for the holiday season

Image: Saks Fifth Ave decorated for the holiday season

Shopping causes hunger...where to pit stop along Fifth Avenue

- **L.A. Burdick**

  5 E 20th St, Manhattan, NY 10003

  While wandering Fifth Avenue on your shopping journey, stop into L.A. Burdick on E. 20th Street for a decadent treat. Their handmade chocolate selections make great gifting options. Be sure to sample their chocolate dipped fruit for a great post lunch treat. Unique treats include chocolate covered matzo.

- **City Bakery**

  3 W 18th St # 1, New York, NY 10011

  Shopping requires a lot of energy, and stopping into City Bakery will give you a much needed refresher! Head west on 18th street right off of 5th Avenue to City Bakery. Styled like a southern cafeteria, City Bakery offers decadent treats like their rich hot chocolate with a wedge of homemade marshmallow in it. Try a pretzel croissant or a blueberry corn muffin, for an unusual but delicious taste bud experience.

- **Madison Square Park**

Take a stroll around Madison Square Park. On the east side of the park is the original Shake Shack, which offers burgers, hotdogs, and original ice cream flavors like Pancakes & Bacon. On early Friday mornings in the summer, free yoga classes are offered, as well as concerts and festivals on the weekends. Look up at the Flatiron Building, one of NYC's oldest and original skyscrapers.

- **Eataly**

200 5th Avenue, New York, NY —

One of the more modern additions to NYC is Eataly. Oscar Farinetti, along with restaurant extraordinaire such as Chef Mario Batali, opened in August 2010. Described by Batali as a "grocery store with tasting rooms", Eataly offers 7 sit down restaurants within the store. Stop into Eataly to explore Italian imported sweets and treats. Head upstairs to *Birreria*, Eataly's year-round rooftop restaurant and beer garden offers family style dishes. Have a glass of wine and look at famous buildings such as the Empire State building in the stylish backdrop. Eataly is also known as a great rooftop bar to mingle, so be sure to keep your eyes out for the next cutie at the bar.

Chapter 8
Holidays in New York City (It's Simply Amazing!)

New York City is an enchanting place during the holidays (end of November to early January). With the exception of the large crowds, there's something magical about that time of the year. Any true New Yorker knows that there is nothing like the smell of the winter chill in the air mixed with Hot Glazed Nuts from the street vendors. Movies like Home Alone have placed their setting during Manhattan's iconic seasonal time. From dazzling window displays to iconic skating rinks, New York City engulfs itself in the season. If you're lucky enough to be able to come during the Holiday Season, here are some of the best Holiday Sights/Activities in New York City to get you in the Holiday Spirit and you cannot miss.

Lighting/Window Displays:

After Thanksgiving through the New Year, famous shopping streets such as Fifth Avenue are transformed into iconic rows: filled with ornate window and lighting displays. From bows to Christmas trees to snowflakes, stores, restaurants, and hotels are covered in dazzling displays. Beware, the weekends and early evenings will be the busiest time. Although the displays can be seen throughout the day, the night is the most magical.

- Macy's in Herald Square is known for their two iconic window displays. The first is set on Broadway between 34th & 35th Streets while the second is along 34th Street. Although the windows change each year, the windows tell the story of the popular stories "Miracle on 34th Street" and "Yes, Virginia".

If heading to the Upper East Side, Bloomingdale's (Lexington between 59th and 60th Streets) is not only another noteworthy shopping destination, but always offer playful and interesting displays. The displays are known to integrate modern technology into the mix, which is fun for the family of all ages. If you're with the family, be sure to stop over at Dylan's Candy Bar nearby on Third Avenue and 60th Street. Started my fashion designer icon Ralph Lauren's daughter Dylan, Dylan's Candy bar boasts three decadent floors of sweet treats and confections. Head to the third floor of the candy bar to the...well bar itself. Sugary sweet cocktails will make you feel like you're in an adult Disney store.

- Like the retail store itself, Barney's New York (Madison Ave between 60th and 61st street) offers contemporary and nontraditional displays.

- Head along Fifth Avenue for couture displays that are sure to impress. Bergdorf Goodman (Fifth Avenue from 58th to 57th Street) stuns with their usual blend of elaborate gowns, breathtaking lights, and Holiday decorations.   Saks Fifth Avenue (Fifth between 49th and 50th) tailors their display to the "child at heart" while Lord & Taylor features traditional holiday displays.

Best Skating Rinks In New York City:

New York City offers pop-up Skating Rinks throughout the city. As soon as the first frost hits (usually early November) to the end of February, the rinks are open from late morning to night. During the Holiday Season, be prepared for long lines and crowded rinks.

- The Rink at Rockefeller Center-30 Rock's Angel Statues, shops, and skating rink make Rockefeller Center top bucket list item to visit during the holidays.

- Bryant Park Skating Rink- Bryant Park is a stone's throw from Times Square. Surprisingly, this famous Midtown location offers free admission with the cost of skates. Celsius, Bryant Park's Pop-up two-floor Holiday themed bar, overlooks the rink. Be sure to take a stroll around the Bryant Park Market for delicious hot chocolate and unique gift ideas.

- Central Park Wollman's Rink-the biggest rink in the city by far, the Wollman rink offers the Midtown skyline in the background while somehow being quiet away from the busy New York traffic.

Insider's Tip: If you plan on ice-skating, try to go during the week around lunchtime. The rinks are less crowded and you'll have to wait less in line. Rates will go up during the weekend as well!

Best Holiday Bar in New York City: Rolfe's German Restaurant

Have you ever wondered what the inside of Christmas tree looked like? Head to Rolfe's German Restaurant in Manhattan's Murray Hill and you won't have to wonder. The restaurant is decked out in garland and holiday decorations. During the holiday season, it offers mulled wine and eggnog: perfect to beat the cool winter temperatures.

Chapters 9-12
New York City's Most Famous Neighborhoods

Any local could spend their entire life explaining what there is to do in New York City. The thing is, it would never stop! There is so much to do in New York and it's constantly changing. Businesses are opening, and some are closing. Some areas become trendy, while others fall off the wagon.

Although New York City hasn't been around thousands of years like international cities such as Rome, Athens, London or Paris, it has packed a lot of history into mere centuries. The skyscrapers, New Year's Eve Ball in Times Square, world-renowned museums, restaurants, and bars, all make it difficult to make a trip to New York City and say you didn't experience anything.

The next chapters of this guidebook dive deeper into some of the core neighborhoods of New York City. Again, if we listed everything to do and see, you wouldn't be able to explore on your own and find some of the best treasures.

How to use the Destination Chapter Listings:

Each listing in the guide is designed to be concise and easy to follow.

- The **travel essentials** section is for orientating yourself in the area.

- **Essential experiences** are the popular, well-known, and well-visited attractions in an area.

- **Noteworthy hidden gems are listed in the destination guide**

- The names of attractions and experiences are **highlighted in bold**.

- Addresses and websites are *provided in the entry*

- The best culinary experiences are detailed in the **where to eat** section. This guide strives to only present good value and good food options. Indicative prices are shown on a scale of **$** (cheap) to **$$$** (very expensive).

- **Where to drink and party** details the kind of vibe to expect in the area, from raucous all night partying to sipping coffee on elegant terraces. The individual listings highlight a few of the best options.

- **Insider's tip** offers a real insight from a local living in the area.

Upper East Side

Travel Essentials:

Located along the east side of famed Central Park, it extends from 59th Street to 96th street. Famous families have spent generations here such as the Kennedys, the Rockefellers, the Roosevelts, and the Carnegies, just to name a few. Today many celebrities call it home. Important museums run along the Upper East Side's section of Fifth Avenue, which is nicknamed the "Museum Mile". This "mile" includes the Metropolitan Museum of Art (www.metmuseum.org/), the Jewish Museum of New York (www.thejewishmuseum.org) , The Frick Collection (www.frick.org), as well as the Guggenheim Museum (www.guggenheim.org), among others. Although the subways run along Lexington Avenue, the MTA Bus line runs down 2nd Avenue, where an array of local known restaurants and pubs are found along the street.

Essential Experiences:

- **Guggenheim Museum-** 1071 Fifth Ave. at 88th St. The building, designed by Frank Lloyd Wright, was designed in the shape of a conch shell. It borders Central Park and offers new exhibits frequently. If you aren't interested in the artwork, at least make your way to see this architecture treasure. www.guggenheim.org.

- **Metropolitan Museum of Art** 1000 Fifth Ave. at 82nd St. Find some of the most amazing pieces of art such as the larger-than-life painting Washington Crossing the Delaware, in the American Wing; the tiny suit of armor of the Infante Luis, Prince of Asturias, in Arms and Armor; and "William," the 12th-dynasty faïence hippo (and Met mascot) in the Egyptian gallery. **Insider's Tip:** If you're feeling thirsty, head to Metropolitan's rooftop bar, which offers stunning views of Central Park. www.metmuseum.org.

- **Gracie Mansion**-Built in 1799 and later restored to its glory, Gracie Mansion became New York's official mayoral residence in 1942. Fun Fact: Gracie Mansion had once served as an ice cream parlor and the first location of the Museum of the City of New York. *General admission is $7 for adults, $4 for seniors, and students are free.*

Where to Eat:

- **$$$-L'Absinthe -** Dubbed as "the best French restaurant in Manhattan,", it offers authentic, turn-of-the century Parisian cuisine is served alongside contemporary French dishes. If not hungry, L'Absinthe Brasserie offers amazing cocktails at their zinc-topped wooden bar. **Main courses range from $23 to $42.**

- **$$-Parlor Steakhouse**-Offering one of the best brunches in New York City, Parlour Steakhouse's Modern American dining

- **$$-Candle 79-**A vegetarian restaurant that offers a menu that's both flavorful and upscale! Try the homemade juices and smoothies. **154 East 79th Street**

- **$$-Hospoda:** This Eastern European contemporary Czech dining option is a stylish spot located on the ground floor of the Bohemian National Hall. Dishes change regularly, and reflect seasonal market.

Have a pint of Pilsner Urquell, poured in four distinct styles ranging from all foam to headless. 321 East 73rd Street

- **$-Delizia 92-**If you want a good slice of American Cheese Pizza, this place is extremely reasonable and the service is friendly. http://www.menupages.com/restaurants/delizia-92/

- **$ Auction House-** 300 E 89th St. This hidden bar doesn't have a website, nor doesn't it even have a sign. The Auction House is a speakeasy style bar with red velvet couches, lux paintings, and smoky lighting. Great to start the night out and see where the locals dwell.

- **$-The Stumble Inn-**Beware of a sea of popped collars and post collegiate frat boys, but embrace the back of bar beer pong tables, low prices, and "stuffed" burgers. They offer a great happy hour and the place is always packed. 1454 2nd Avenue, NY, NY 10021, corner of 76th Street

- **The Penrose-** if you're into happy houring with attractive people and meeting locals, the fact that they have good food and drinks is only a bonus. 1590 2nd Avenue

- **The Met Rooftop Bar-**In the summer, it's really hard to beat this: amazing park views, art, a sense of escaping, and a sense of drinking with the skyline in the backdrop. Metropolitan Museum of Art.

Upper West Side

The iconic Upper West Side is known for its "old money" roots and high end suits. From baby strollers to dog walkers, the Upper West Side is indeed the most family oriented of the more popular Manhattan neighborhoods. Traditional grey stone buildings line the streets with picturesque views. Many of the most expensive retail shopping is available in this area, along with quiet tree strewn streets and local bakeries. Keep an eye out for celebrities, as many prefer this posh and quiet neighborhood. The Lincoln Center for the Arts, prestigious Columbus Circle, and satellite classrooms to the prestigious

Fordham University and Columbia University can be found in the Upper West Side.

Experience Essentials:

- **American Museum of Natural History** Central Park West at 79th St. The movie *The Night at the* Museum didn't do it justice. Check out the Cosmic Pathway in the Rose Center for Earth and Space, the dinosaur halls, and the blue whale in the Hall of Ocean Life. There's also a new food court. www.amnh.org.

- **Whitney Museum of American Art** 945 Madison Ave. at 75th St. Check out Alexander Calder's Circus, on the fifth floor, as well as the film in which the artist plays all of the roles. www.whitney.org.

- **Children's Museum of Manhattan** 212 W. 83rd St. A Peanuts exhibit lets kids crawl into Snoopy's house, play Schroeder's piano, and even take a turn at Lucy's psychiatry booth. www.cmom.org.

- **Strawberry Fields-**72nd Street and Central Park West- Strawberry Fields is a 2.5-acre landscaped section in New York City's Central Park dedicated to the memory of former Beatle John Lennon.

Where to Eat:

- **$-Levain Bakery**- Be expected to wait in a line, but trust us, it's worth it. Their chocolate walnut cookies are out of this world.

- **$-Jacques Torres**-If you've ever wondered what the inside of Willy Wonka's factory may have looked like or smelled like, then step into Jacque Torres. Try the Mexican hot chocolate for an unexpected spicy kick to the classic warm drink.

- **$-Blockheads**- 951 Amsterdam Avenue. Burritos the size of your plate and $4 margaritas. Need we go on??

- **$$- Jacob's Pickles -** Pickles are the bedrock of this sprawling and fun-loving café, inspired to look like an old-fashioned Jewish deli, and the pickles end up in nearly everything. The breakfast and ridiculously large biscuit sandwiches are not to be missed. 509 Amsterdam Avenue

- **$$-The Dead Poet**-450 Amsterdam Avenue #1, New York, NY 10024. This bar will please any literary nerd as the cocktails are named after dead writers and poets. They're hauntingly good.

- **$-Prohibition**-The Jazz Themed Bar offers a long cocktail list and live band performances nightly. 503 Columbus Avenue, New York, NY 10024

- **$-Dive 75**- 101 West 75th Street, New York, NY 10023. This bar isn't as divey as you would expect from the name, but offers a large menu of drinks, board games, and you drink your beers out of a fish tank

Chapter 10
Midtown Manhattan

Midtown

Travel Essentials:

If looking for New York City's renowned bright lights and city hustle, then head to Midtown. This small neighborhood is not to be judged by size, as its streets are home to some of the most well known buildings such as Chrysler Building, Grand Central, and the Empire State Building, and the iconic Bryant Park. Be sure to look at the New Year's Eve Ball and the bright billboards in Times Square (http://www.timessquarenyc.org/index.aspx). Between 44th and 52nd street you will find the Theater District, which holds many popular Broadway and theater shows. Walk along the shops of 5th Avenue, stop into the famous MoMA (www.moma.org), as well as Radio City Music Hall (www.radiocity.com), and Rockefeller Center (www.rockefellercenter.com).

Experience Essentials:

- **The Paley Center for Media 25 W. 52nd St www.paleycenter.org**

- **Museum of Modern Art 11 West 53rd St.** Modern art exhibits feature iconic impressionist painters such as Van Gogh to modern street art. **www.moma.org.**

- **Times Square** (42nd St. and Broadway) has been transformed in recent years from seedy to slick, an inevitably controversial makeover. There's no arguing, however, that its extravagant kilowattage is energizing. Can you imagine the electric bill?

- **Rockefeller Center** (48th to 51st Sts., between Fifth Ave. and Ave. of the Americas; 212/632-3975; www.rockefellercenter.com), an architectural phoenix that rose during the Depression, is home to NBC and the Today show studio, and named after one of the most iconic families. The skating rink is open October to April, and Paul Marship's shining sculpture of Prometheus stands next to it.

- **Grand Central Terminal** (42nd to 45th Sts., between Vanderbilt and Lexington Aves www.grandcentralterminal.com), after a tedious restoration, this famous terminal has become a destination in itself. There are shops and restaurants, even a food court—none of which has sullied its image as an architectural masterpiece. Look up in the Main Concourse with its celestial ceiling (look for a tiny patch of dark gray—the before-cleaning color—in the northwest corner).

Where to Eat:

- **$-NumPang Sandwich Shop**-This sandwich shop adds Cambodian flavors for an unusual but flavorful sandwich. Our pick is the ginger brisket.

- **$$-Burger Joint**-To really feed your beef addiction, try this hidden gem, tucked behind a wall of curtains in Le Parker Meridien—a bit pricier but a cool spot to scarf a burger. **Insider's Tip:** They take cash only and there is a long line.

- **$$$**-Le Bernandin-True authentic French cuisine at a revered restaurant in Midtown. http://www.le-bernardin.com

- **$$$-Vitae**-Using the freshest ingredients, Vitae is all about seasonal and farm to market options. From the creamy homemade burrata cheese to roasted duck, you'll dine in culinary heaven http://www.vitaenyc.com

- **$$$-Del Frisco's**-Rockefeller Center-This American Steakhouse is a favorite. It offers master made mixologist cocktails and mouthwatering desserts to boot. delfriscos.com

- **$- Blue Bottle Coffee-Rockefeller Center,** 1 Rockefeller Plaza, New York, NY 10020 This upscale coffeehouse offers coffee drinks & pastries, freshly roasted beans, and souvenir mugs.

Insider's Tips:

- Some of the cheapest prices for Broadway and Off-Broadway tickets can be at a TKTS Booth. These are typically 25-50% off full-price, meaning you'll pay about $60-$85 per ticket, instead of the regular $100+. If you are a student, head to the show theater itself for student rates.

- Saunter up either 6th or 7th Avenue for more "pop culture" landmarks such as the Late Night Theater, Rockefeller Center, and the entrance of Central Park.

- The Times Square Alliance offers daily updated information regarding specials, discounts, and events going on in Times Square. Although many New Yorkers do not take advantage of it, head to this site to find specials and discounts on a wide range of events from happy hours to lunch specials to activities http://www.timessquarenyc.org/deals/index.aspx#.VAYrVvYiq4I

- Use location-based apps such as Yelp or OpenTable to help you find restaurants and the best happy hour around Times Square. Don't be afraid if it takes you off track to 8th Avenue or 9th Avenue (Hell's Kitchen). Some of the best Italian and Thai food is featured there, as well as great Happy Hour specials that are more reasonable than the tourist prices of Times Square. OpenTable offers you the option to reserve a table before you get to the restaurant, so you won't lost time sight-seeing

- Times Square is known for both its lights and stores. The stores are known to have a wider shopping assortment to accommodate the traffic and compete with other stores.   Some of the stores, such as the Toys "R" Us , which features an indoor Ferris wheel. On 48th Street and Broadway, Hershey's Chocolate World offers NYC themed sweets right across the street from M&M's World. Walt Disney World's flagship store features a Barbie condo on the second floor, and is themed to lead you through the Enchanted Forest.

- If you plan on spending time in Times Square for New Year's Eve, make sure to get there early. As it becomes more crowded, NYPD starts barricading people in organized sections. You won't be able to eat, drink, use the bathroom, or leave the area. It is very cold in December, and you should plan to dress according.

- **When traveling in or around popular tourist attractions, here are some Tourist DON'Ts:**

1. Do not walk three people across. Two is the limit. The streets are filled with tourists, locals, and cultural acts. When you stop in the middle of the road to take a picture, you're disrupting the flow of walking traffic. To avoid being called out by a local, respect people's limited space.

2. If a mascot or character (such as the Naked Cowboy) walks up to you and your group, you do NOT have to take a picture with them. If you do, they will ask for money.

3. Hold tight to your phone/camera. In the busy streets, it's easy to get bumped into, and even easier to drop them.

4. Do not stand in the busy streets of New York City to take photos. The cabs and people both have places to go, and with the traffic, it makes them harder to stop. Head to the red bleachers above the TKTS Booth in Times Sqaure to take the best photo at a higher view.

Where to Drink and Party:

- **$$-The Rum House**-Don Jose, the head bartender, knows to make an island drink like no other. Sip on a drink and dream of being on an island far away. 228 W 47th St

- **$$-Cask Bar & Grill**-167 E 33rd St . This is a local's hang out and revered bar. This dim lit gastro pub offers delicious appetizers like flatbreads and homemade mac & cheese.

- **$$-Sofia Wine Bar & Café**- 242 E 50th St. One of the best places for happy hour.

- **$$$-The Campbell Apartment**-Grand Central Terminal, 15 Vanderbilt Ave -This 1920s themed cocktail bar is another hidden gem that is worthy of your trip. The jazz and swing music sets the mood.

- **$$$-Bar 44-Royalton Hotel, 44 E. 44th Street**-If you're looking for an upscale, swanky hotel bar where you'll see a celebrity sighting or two, Bar 44 is your place. Not to mention, they grow the cocktail herbs in house for the freshest ingredients.

Hell's Kitchen

Due to the large corporations and tourist attractions like Times Square, you will find your most expensive options for dining and nightlife in Midtown. Popular chains and retail stores reside closer to Times Square. If you're traveling on a budget or looking for local cuisine, walk west to 9th Avenue in Midtown to the Hell's Kitchen neighborhood. Hell's Kitchen, also known as Clinton or the Midtown West neighborhood, is located between 34th to 59th street, between Eighth Avenue and the Hudson River. "Restaurant Row" is located between 8th and 9th Avenue in Hell's Kitchen. Hell's Kitchen is known for its nightlife and supportive gay culture.

Experience Essentials:

- **Hell's Kitchen Flea Market-** 39th St. betw. Ninth & Tenth Aves. Over 100 vendors set up on 39th street. With a little digging you may find your diamond in the rough.

- **Intrepid Sea, Air & Space Museum,** Pier 86, Twelfth Ave. at 46th St. Easy to get to by subway, walking or cab, the complex boasts authentically restored aircraft, USS Growler (the only guided missile submarine in the world that's open to the public), a British Airways Concorde, and the Space Shuttle Pavilion, featuring Enterprise.

Where to Eat:

- **$$-Becco-**Mouthwatering Italian just like grandma used to make it. http://becco-nyc.com/

- **$$-La Pulperia-**Authentic Latin American and fresh cocktails. Perfect for a spring/summer outside dinner. www.pulperianyc.com

- **$$$-Oceana-**This quaint stop in Restaurant Row offers out of this world seafood dishes and homemade pasta. (http://www.oceanarestaurant.com/

- **$-Pio, Pio-**Purvian food at its finest. Your meal comes buffet style with fixings. Perfect for a group outing.

Where to Drink and Party:

- **$-Pony Bar-$5 Beers.** Cheese covered tater tots. One of the best single bars to mingle on the Westside. Need we go on? 637 10th Avenue, New York, NY 10036
- **$-Landsdowne Road-**This quaint Irish Pub is where the locals hang while watching a game on TV. Their chicken wings are some of the best in the city. 599 10th Avenue, New York, NY 10036

- **$$-Southern Hospitality-**Justin Timberlake's famed southern styled bar is highly recommended for brunch. The restaurant offers bottomless mimosas, bloody marys, and bellinis with hangover helping dishes like Huevos Rancheros or Fried Chicken. Great to hang out on a rainy day and meet locals. 45 9th Avenue, New York, NY 10036

- **Atlas Social Club-743 Ninth Avenue** This retro-sports-themed gay bar and club offers fun two-for-one drink specials during happy hour, vintage boxing posters line the walls, and dancing goes on until late at night.

Chapter 11
Lower Manhattan

Experience Essentials:

- **Lower East Side Tenement Museum-**90 Orchard St In this building, which was home to 10,000 people from 20 nations between 1863 and 1935, don't miss the quarters of famed Prussian dressmaker Natalie Gumpertz, who shared the quarters with her four children.www.tenement.org.

- **Union Square-**located at where Broadway and Fourth Avenue intersect, this famous Park, restaurant row, and shopping area is not to be missed. During the summer months, they offer a Farmer's market comprised of local fresh goods. In the holidays, they have a Christmas market set up with unique gifting options.

- **9/11 Memorial-**Pay Homage to those that lost their lives in the 9/11 Terrorist Attacks, at the beautiful memorial which is now two infinity pools in the locations of the previous World Trade Centers

Lower East Side

Travel Essentials:

The Lower East Side is seen as one of the "trendier" areas of New York. It's shorter buildings, street graffiti, street vendors, and laid-back vibe are a far cry from looking like the tall cityscape of Midtown. Whether in the mood for a quick bite at the famous Katz's Deli (www.katzsdelicatessen.com), or strolling the streets to view the street art, the LES filled with buzzing restaurants and bars The LES has become a popular neighborhood for nightlife. Music venues such as Bowery Electric (www.theboweryelectric.com), or the Mercury Lounge (www.mercuryloungenyc.com offer live shows daily. Orchard and Ludlow have become popular streets for dancing, martinis, and lounges.

Where to Eat:

- **$-Sao Mai-** Their Pho tai is out of this world and the locals know it. Extremely flavorful broth, beef thin and rare, the noodles are homemade and light.

- **$-Zucker Bakery-**Oogle at this bakery's large assortment of sweets and treats. **Insider's Tip:** Their alfajores cookies (dulce de leche filled cookie sandwich rolled in coconut flakes) are something to write home to mom about. Zukerbakery.com

- **$$-China North Dumpling-**From the homemade kimchi to homemade dumplings, anything goes in this delicious eatery.

- **$$-Stanton Social-This 3 level space takes eclectic to a new level.** Decadent gourmet small plates, high-end cocktails & music make this a chic, trendy spot. 99 Stanton Street, New York, NY 10002

Where to Drink and Party:

- **$-Spitzer's Corner Bar-**Great place to mingle. Get lost in the variety of beers on tap. www.spitzerscorner.com

- **$$-Fat Baby-**Dance the night away at Fat Baby. With an eclectic array of music, you'll be sure to break a sweat www.fatbabynyc.com **Insider's Tip:** Get there before midnight to avoid paying an expensive cover charge.

- **$-National Underground-**Offers daily live music shows. Owned by recorded artist Gavin DeGraw, this venue always holds interesting artists and open mic opportunities. www.thenationalunderground.com

- **$-Mehanata Bulgarian Bar-**This bar is one of the craziest options in New York City, and is not for the faint at heart. From the ice bar where you can drink as many shots as you can in 2 minutes to the stripper poles and loud pumping music, it's always guaranteed to be a good time.   http://www.mehanata.com/

East Village

If you're looking for something a little off the beaten path, the East Village is for you. Don't be weary of the graffiti signed walls. Instead, bask in the freedom of art. The East Village is known for its vibrant history in the arts. For the cocktail aficionado, bask in the days of bowtie wearing bartenders, smoky hidden rooms, and moody music playing in the background as you head to a "secret" speakeasy. They won't be easy to track down, but once you find such symbols such as an unmarked door leading to these spots, you'll have an adventure and a cocktail to talk about for life. If looking for nightlife, the East Village is thriving.

Experience Essentials:

- Sing your heart out at a karaoke bar along St. Mark's Place

- Ponder at getting a tattoo by some of the most famous tattoo artists along eclectic St. Marks Place

- Head to speakeasy and get a fabulous cocktail

Where to Eat:

- **$$-Back Forty**-190 Ave B This higher scale gastro pub offers seasonal-eats tavern, where farmhouse chic prevails in the dining room (vintage tools adorn the walls) and on the menu. www.backforty.com

- **$-Pommes Frites**-123 2nd Avenue. If you're wondering why there is a wait around the block, it's because you've come to Pommes Frites. They offer twice fried potatoes with a variety of dipping sauces from spicy to sweet.

- **$$-Desnuda**-This quaint wine and tapas bar offers amazing selections of food and drinks. 122 E. 7th Street

Where to Drink and Party:

- **$$$-Little Branch**-The unmarked door of Little Branch disguises the cocktail Jazz bar from most tourists. Once entered, you'll be surprised to find the warm and inviting atmosphere, master mixologists, reminiscent of the days of prohibition era glamour. littlebranch.net

- **$-The 13th Step**-Like the Upper East Side's Big Brother, The Stumble Inn, The 13th Step is known for their frat culture, packed bar, and high energy nightlife 149 2nd Avenue, New York, NY 10003

- **$-McSorley's Ale House** will quench your thirst. Established in 1854, McSorley's became an institution by remaining a steadfast authentic Irish Pub and providing only two choices to its customers: McSorley's Dark Ale and McSorley's Light Ale. The best part? It's always buy one pint get one pint free.

- **$$-Angel's Share**-Another speakeasy makes our list and may be hard to find, but it's worth the treasure hunt. 8 Stuyvesant Street, New York, NY 10003

- **$$$-PDT (Please Don't Tell)**-This cocktail bar is one of the more unique hidden speakeasies in New York. Hidden inside a telephone booth in Criff Dog's Hot Dog Restaurant, a hostess opens the door to take your reservation. You may have to wait but you'll be thankful you took the time to check out the taxidermy-laden walls and bartender concoctions http://pdtnyc.com/

SoHo

Travel Essentials:

SoHo is known for its eclectic shopping, art galleries, and restaurants. The cobblestone streets offer landmark cast iron buildings, which hold some of the most unique shopping in the world. Whether looking for local boutiques, chain retail stores, or high-end items, SoHo has every shop you could want. Wander through popular ethnic areas such as Chinatown or Little Italy to get a true taste of authentic cuisine.

Experience Essentials:

- Grab a cannoli in Little Italy

- Walk through Chinatown and haggle for goods (Insider's Tip: Do NOT walk through the Fish Market in the summer. You will regret it)

Where to Eat:

- $$-**La Mela**-One of the best Italian restaurants in Little Italy. Be sure to look at the celebrities wall to see all who have dined there.(http://www.lamelarestaurant.com)

- $$-**Balthazar's**-Traditional bistro fare style restaurant, and one of the best breakfasts in New York City (http://www.balthazarny.com/),

- $$$-**Mercer Kitchen** (http://www.themercerkitchen.com) A celebrity favorite, this restaurant offers relaxed seating and upscale dining

Where to Drink and Party:

SoHo is also known for its nightlife, which ranges from wine bars to swanky upscale lounge.

- **$$-Canal Room**-If you're looking to dance the night away, the Canal Room is a good place to go and mingle www.canalroom.com

- **$$$-MercBar**-offering outstanding seasonal martinis, this bar captures the swanky upscale nature of SoHo www.mercbar.com

- **$$$-Thompson Hotel Bar-**The master mixologists are some of the best in the world. Ask them to make bartender's choice of cocktail. We dare you. www.thompsonhotels.com/hotels/nyc/60-thompson

Chapter 12
Brooklyn and Queens

Brooklyn-Williamsburg

Travel Essentials:

The rapidly growing Brooklyn area of Williamsburg has a lot to offer if you're willing to take the journey. The easiest access is by subway. The redefined Williamsburg area will likely surprise you, as its recycled and renovated industrial buildings hold new apartment buildings and local businesses. Giving more of a suburb atmosphere than city, this area is a breath of fresh air from the "big island". For the adventurous type, head to Bedford Avenue off the L train for a variety of locally owned boutiques (such as the acclaimed Minimarket   http://www.timeout.com/newyork/shopping/miniminimarket), kitschy restaurants, and street vendors. Walk along the water's edge to get a great view of the Manhattan cityscape.

Where to Eat:

- **$$-Sweet Chick-**The Southern meets modern elements of this restaurant are different, and the locals love it. Try a watermelon martini or lemon waffle. sweetchicknyc.com

- **$$$-Delaware and Hudson-**New to the restaurant scene, this prestigious culinary experience has already earned a Michelin Star. delawareandhudson.com

- **$$-Shalom Japan-**When you first think of the title, you think "No can it really be Japanese and Jewish food?" Why yes, yes it can. And it works so well. 310 S. 4th Street

- **$$-Rye-247 S. 1st Street.** From amazing brunch, to mastery craft cocktails and a truly unique dining experience, it's easy to see why this restaurant has a cult following

Where to Drink and Dance:

- **$-Brooklyn Brewery-**The first and most famous brewery in the New York City area offers tours and tastings www.brooklynbrewery.com

- **$$-Brooklyn Bowl-**If looking or a fun rainy day activity or just want to listen to live music, head to Brooklyn Bowl (around the corner from Brooklyn Brewery), where you'll be able to bowl, drink local brews, and eat acclaimed bites

- **$-The Commodore-**366 Metropolitan Ave –This dive bar offers old arcade games, the best fried drunk food, loud music, and hipster local watching

- **Union Pool-**Another seedy dive bar on the list, this former pool supply outlet now offers an outdoor bar, music venue, and fun atmosphere. $3 Beers and $5 Mix drinks on most days that end in –y. Beware, you're in hipster territory. http://union-pool.com

- **The Whiskey Brooklyn-**44 Berry Street. This underground half dance club/half bar ensures sweaty good times, a hangover, and phone numbers written on your hand.

Queens

Travel Essentials:

There are so many neighorhoods in Brooklyn and Queens that it's hard to keep up with! Astoria, Queens is one of the fastest growing cities due to its close proximity and delicious food. Known for its strong Greek heritage, Beer Garden, and vibrant bakeries, this neighborhood will be a memorable detour on your journey.

Where to Eat:

- **$-La Guli-**2915 Ditmars, close to 31st St and the final stop of the N subway. The fresh cannoli will haunt your dreams for years to come.

- **$$-Tavern Kyclades-**This restaurant treats Greek food as an art form. 33-07 Ditmars Boulevard, Queens, NY 11105

- **SSS-Water's Edge-**401 44th Drive, Long Island City, NY This upscale Modern American dining offers extraordinary views of the Manhattan skyline

Where to Drink and Dance:

- **$$-Bohemia Beer Garden, Astoria Queens-**The only old-school, big beer garden left in New York City, Turn off crazy urban 31st Street-- the subway overhead-and escape into a huge beer garden with its shady trees, picnic tables, pitchers of icy beer, and platters of hearty Czech food and summer barbecue. It's a must on summer weekends with live folk music on many afternoons. Bohemia Beer Garden is a true urban oasis and a local favorite.

- **$$$-Dutch Kills-**27-24 Jackson Avenue, Long Island City, -This Long Island City bar has a speakeasy feel. Get lost in the upscale cocktails and skyline view.

- **$$-LIC Bar-**45-58 Vernon Boulevard, Long Island City, If you're looking to hang with the locals, you've found your place.

Conclusion
See You in the Big Apple!

Thanks for reading the guidebook. We mean it! Your eyes and interest keep us writing these insightful guidebooks, and without you there wouldn't be a reason to creepily lurk from street to street to get the inside scoop.

What was your favorite part about New York? Which story will be shared for years to come? Was there a meal you'll hopelessly think about and recommend to all who are visiting? Or, was there a moment where you truly felt like a "New Yorker"?

Did our guidebooks help you? We hope you saved some money, laughed at some of our snarky New York comments, and enjoyed the piece of Pizza that may have tasted like heaven.

Whatever you did in New York City, we like to think that this guidebook has gave you the tools and insightful information to add to your tourism experience. From knowing where the best cannolis were in Queens to getting that bottomless brunch in Hell's Kitchen, our insider's tips come from those who have lived and breathed New York, and can call it their home. Hopefully it showed you the tourist spots you were hoping to see, the amazing pictures you'll always keep, and the hidden gems that you'll never forget.

We're always looking to improve our guidebooks. If this guidebook wasn't helpful then let us know why. There's no point writing if it's not helpful to visitors. We won't take it personally. Furthermore, because this is an electronic book, we know it's not going to end up in the bin. Likewise, if there's something you really liked then we want to know about it.

Thanks again for reading. Again, don't take the New York Attitude offensive.

We really are good people…especially when there's a martini in our hands. But don't talk bad about our Yankees or our mothers…ever.

Until next time!

Dagny Taggart

Learn Any Language 300% FASTER

>> Get Full Online Language Courses With Audio Lessons <<

Would you like to learn a new language before you start your trip? I think that's a great idea. Now, why don't you do it 300% *FASTER*?

I've partnered with the most revolutionary language teachers to bring you the very language online courses I've ever seen. It's a mind-blowing program specifically created for language hackers such as ourselves. It will allow you learn ANY language, from French to Chinese, 3x faster, straight from the comfort of your own home, office, or wherever you may be. It's like having an unfair advantage!

You can choose from a wide variety of languages, such as French, Spanish, Italian, German, Chinese, Portuguese, and A TON more.

Each Online Course consists of:

+ 91 Built-In Lessons
+ 33 Interactive Audio Lessons
+ 24/7 Support to Keep You Going

The program is extremely engaging, fun, and easy-going. You won't even notice you are learning a complex foreign language from scratch. And before you realize it, by the time you go through all the lessons you will officially become a truly solid speaker.

Old classrooms are a thing of the past. It's time for a revolution.

If you'd like to go the extra mile, then follow the link below, and let the revolution begin!

>> http://bitly.com/foreign-language-courses <<

CHECK OUT THE COURSE »

PS: Can I Ask You a Quick Favor?

If you liked the book, please leave a nice review on Amazon! I'd absolutely love to hear your feedback. Every time I read your reviews... you make me smile. I'd be immensely thankful if you go to Amazon now, and write down a quick line sharing with me your experience. I personally read ALL the reviews there, and I'm thrilled to hear your feedback and honest motivation. It's what keeps me going, and helps me improve everyday =)

Please go Amazon now and drop a quick review sharing your experience!

***

THANKS!

***

ONCE YOU'RE BACK,
FLIP THE PAGE!
BONUS CHAPTER AHEAD
=)

Introduction
Are You Ready for an Amazing Journey?

Welcome to London. Welcome to a city of eccentricity, lauded throughout world history and throbbing with the iconic and the alternative. Black taxis, red buses, famous clocks, flashing skyscrapers, wine bars tucked down labyrinthine alleys...and that's all within an hour of landing in this chaotic capital. London is mad. From the throngs that gather on tiny Trafalgar Square to the disused toilet cubicles turned into coffee joints, there's something peculiar and bizarre at every turn. Even the breakfasts don't look real; is it really possible to start your day with six *different* fried foods? Mugs of tea with milk, pints of "real ale," opulent shopping experiences, grubby atmospheric basements, glorious architectural relics, or graffiti ridden streets...welcome to London and welcome to an incomparable travel experience.

But which side of London are you going to see? Perhaps the funky neighborhoods of the East, bursting with vibrant color and pop-up markets. Maybe the elegant townhouses of the West, standing proud in all their Victorian splendor. Of course, few want to miss out on the bright and famous; Buckingham Palace, Piccadilly Circus, Oxford Street theater, Westminster flickering over the River Thames... London's greatest appeal is its diversity. In the space of just two Underground stops you will travel to another borough, a disparate entity in the overarching sphere that calls itself London. Most Londoners never even venture into the center, stoically sticking to the sights of their own local borough. Likewise, most tourists never venture out of Underground Zone 1, missing out on the rich tapestry of culture and experiences that await in the outlying boroughs.

It would take a few generations to understand London and everything it has to offer. Even the most longstanding of "cockney" locals wouldn't claim to know it all. London for tourists has two distinct sides. Initially, there's the essential and the iconic, all the famous sights and experiences that grace television screens around the world. It's hard to visit London and miss these global travel icons. But London is undeniably bigger than this. There's a very local side, discovered all over the city and delivering thick doses of originality and charm. For tourists, this is the alternative side, the patchwork of idiosyncrasies that make London such an unforgettable experience. This guidebook celebrates both, ensuring you don't miss out on the iconicity, but you also soak up the authentic and intimate side to this buzzing metropolis. Of course, the guide is written by a Londoner; who else would be qualified for such a job? But it's also filled with insider tips from locals living in different boroughs.

So jump into London as we explain it all, from where to sleep to where to grab a 3am snack, how to use the public transport to how to spend less and experience more. This guidebook isn't thick on history or background information. So there isn't four pages on the detailed history of Westminster; that can all be discovered when you visit the ancient parliament. Instead, this guidebook is rich in practical information and ideas that enable you to craft an individualized London experience. Think of it as the friendly local in your pocket, offering directions, suggestions, and essential knowledge. It won't tell you what to do. But it will ensure you have all the information to create your own perfect London vacation.

Here's a quick rundown of the guide for easy reference.

- **Chapter 2 - Understanding London**: A brief overview of London from a visitor's perspective, helping you get your bearings and understand the different areas of the city.

- **Chapter 3 – Essential London Experiences and Trip Planning**: This chapter starts with a rundown of the best of London, both for its famous sights and unknown attractions. There's something for all eventualities, including what to do on an infamous rainy day. It's all followed with some succinct information about planning an itinerary and when to go.

- **Chapter 4 – Where to Sleep:** From £10 dorm beds to £1000+ five star luxury, London has something for every taste. This chapter covers it all and includes individual listings of the best London has to offer.

- **Chapter 5 – How to use London's Public Transport:** Nobody drives in London so you're going to have to get to grips with the network of underground lines and bus services.

- **Chapter 6 - How to Travel Smart, Experience More, and Spend Less:** London regular appears in the top echelons of the world's most expensive cities. But you don't need to max out three credit cards to experience London. This chapter helps take the spending out of the stratosphere.

- **Chapters 7 - 11:** These sections provide rich detail about the individual boroughs. They're packed with insider's tips, essential sights, uncovered attractions, where to eat, drink, party, and how to experience the borough from a local perspective.

- **Chapter 12: See you in London!** A brief conclusion and thank you.

Chapter 1
London at a Glance (North, South, East, West)

Map 1: London at a Glance

To understand London it's essential to deconstruct. You probably think of London as a big capital city. Which it is...from a distance. Get up close and London is a patchwork of individual villages, or boroughs as they're locally known. For over 1000 years, each has been developing separately and organically. Take a look at the map and check out the names; traveling between any two of them is like traveling to a new city. Chelsea is regal and grand, full of luxuriant shopping experiences and Michelin star dining. Head a few miles south and you're in Brixton, a place of dingy basement clubs and vivid graffitied streets. Most of the famous attractions are packed into a tiny area in the very heart of the city, covering boroughs like the City of London and South Bank in millions of camera wielding tourists.

Each has its own attractions, both iconic and alternative, and each has its own appeal. Some boroughs are for partying, others for strolling hand in hand along graceful streets. Being in London is like visiting dozens of different destinations, each held together by the arteries of the city; the London Underground. While Londoners enthusiastically complain about public transport, they don't realize how good they've got it. Everywhere is connected and chapter five of this guide provides detailed information on how to effectively use London's public transport.

Understanding London's Different Regions

As much as each borough is different, there are some overarching geographical similarities. For the visitor, London can be loosely divided into five areas; East, North, South, West, and Central. Simple huh? Certainly more simple that working out which beer to order at a traditional London pub. Each has a vastly different appeal and history, so here's a quick lowdown.

Central London

The delight of every first time visitor, Central London is where you'll discover all the iconic sights that have danced across your television screen for the last however many years. It's   swarming with tourists. But it's quite brilliant. In just a couple of hours you can walk from Buckingham Palace to Westminster, across to St Paul's Cathedral, over London Bridge, around the renowned banking district and then onto Oxford Street. Save plenty of space on your memory card as a day in Central London bursts with infamous photo opportunities. However, Central London is horribly expensive, the prices soaring via the uncomfortable marriage of bankers and tourists. A bad cafe lunch for two won't provide much change from £30.

Most Londoners rarely visit the center, put off by both the prices and the crowds. You also won't find much in the way of atmosphere or culture here. However, it's unmissable for tourists for a couple of reasons. There's simply too many incredible sights to ignore, even if some don't quite live up to the hype. Furthermore, Central London is, well, very *central*. So as you explore the city you're likely to cross through this area on a daily basis, particularly as it's where to find the major transport hubs.

Two black taxis outside St Paul's Cathedral, a symbol of Central London's iconicity.

East London

Have you heard of cockney rhyming slang? Or Londoners that speak with a thick indecipherable accent? Phrases like "apples and pears" meaning "stairs," or "dog and bone" translating to "telephone." East London is the city's historic working class roots, full of pride and tradition. It's where you'll find "cockneys," huge markets, atmospheric pubs, and boroughs full of delight and intrigue. Although it's becoming increasingly gentrified by "hipsters" from the city, the East remains a thoroughly original and alternative side to London.

East London is all about experiences, from vintage second hand shopping stalls to boutique pop-up restaurants and the sound of buskers emanating from beneath train bridges. Young visitors will be in their element, as it's packed with the city's best places to party. It's also great for anyone with time to explore, as the best sights are often tucked away. East London is the cheapest side of London, so if you don't mind the slightly grubby facade, spending more time here will do wonders for your budget. The major downside is that the London Underground doesn't reach that far into the region, so public transport isn't as easy as elsewhere.

North London

Leafy North London is the city's more serene side, full of the pleasant and charming. It's got the graceful aesthetics that sooth the soul and the relaxed atmosphere that pleases the heart. Expect to find great restaurants, hundreds of outstanding places to drink, quirky organic food markets, and a real taste of middle class London that hasn't been hit by the bulldozer. Transport connections are excellent and the prices are reasonable, making North London the best value choice for accommodation.

You won't find scores of attractions, although it's easy to stay occupied. For example, just walking along Stoke Newington's high street can take a few hours as you dip into cute cafes and charming second hand book shops. The local residents are a particularly proud bunch, often refusing to travel anywhere "south of the river." North London doesn't have the excitement of elsewhere; great if you're wanting to avoid crowds but not the best for all night partying.

West London

Home to the rich and famous and proud of its astronomical real estate prices, West London is the aristocratic side to the city. Wide streets are overlooked by gorgeous Victorian townhouses, shopping centers have an extravagant opulence, and there's more green space than anywhere else in London. When the world's top fashion brands say they have a store in London, they mean they have store in West London. It's an area for boutique shopping, exceptional fine dining, gorgeous architecture, and needing to dress to impress.

West London will blow a hole in almost every budget, the difference to Central London being that you're getting something unique for your money. So while a dinner for two might cost £100 it's going to be outstanding food. The area has great transport connections so taking trips out to the West is easy to add into any day's itinerary. This is London at its grand and glorious best, complete with yuppies (you might call them "preppies") and residents with serious wads of cash.

South London

The city's least visited part lies south of the River Thames, a hotchpotch of working class neighborhoods, sprouting financial districts, and one of the planet's most diverse populations. Some might call it a city upon itself, others could say it's a dozen individual cities with no relation to the next. Still more will claim that it lacks an identity. However, those prepared to cross the Thames will explore a misunderstood and vastly different side to the city.

Young people wanting to get off the beaten track will love boroughs like Brixton and Clapham, home to all night parties and a thick undercurrent of the underground. Wandering away from the Thames brings a mixture of converted warehouses and gleaming new skyscrapers. It's an affordable part of the city and transport connections are good, although a little slow.

Understanding London's Culture

London is probably the easiest city in the world to blend in. Home to over 200 different nationalities and who knows how many native languages, the city is an amalgamation of ideas and personalities, shaped on a daily basis by an evocative blend of competing cultures. Other than having your face in a map, or wielding a telescopic camera lens, there's little that will make you stand out. Staunch right wingers will say that almost everyone in London is a visitor and the city's original roots have been lost. But that's just ideological nonsense. London is all the better for this thick coating of random influence.

Looking confused in front of a metro map, or standing in awe at a monument, also doesn't mark you out as a tourist. London has a transient population, with a large proportion of its residents spending a few years in the "big smoke" before moving elsewhere. So expect to meet local residents in the most famous of museums. Swapping tales about homelands and backgrounds is something you'll be doing on a regular basis, whether it's in a small cafe or black taxi.

Many guidebooks can be filled with what to eat, drink, how to colloquially say hello, and which cultural faux pas's to avoid. But what is traditional London food anyway? The fried breakfast at your Bed and Breakfast or the Indian Curry on Brick Lane? Sausage rolls or Lebanese buffets? There's no need to get hung up on customs or etiquette. Just be yourself and enjoy the experience.

To Check out the Rest of "*London For Tourists*" go to Amazon and Look For It Right Now!

LONDON
For Tourists

The Traveler's Guide to Make the Most Out of Your
Trip to London - Where to Go, Eat, Sleep & Party

DAGNY TAGGART

Check Out My Other Books

Are you ready to exceed your limits? Then pick a book from the one below and start learning yet another new language.   I can't imagine anything more fun, fulfilling, and exciting!

If you'd like to see the entire list of language guides (there are a ton more!), go to:

>>**http://www.amazon.com/Dagny-Taggart/e/B00K54K6CS/**<<

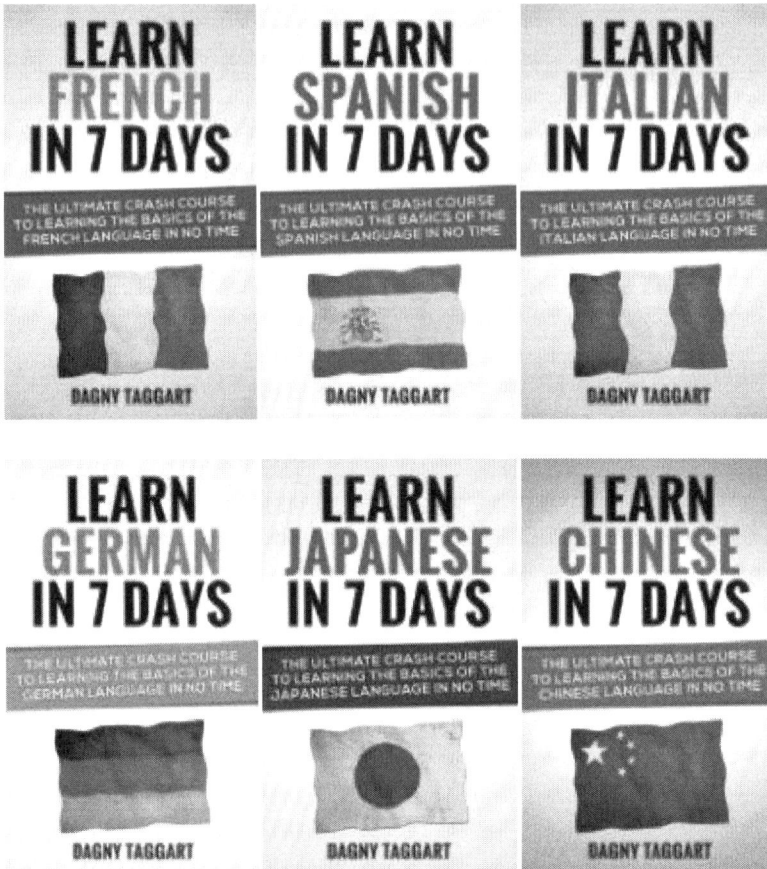

About the Author

Dagny Taggart is a language enthusiast and polyglot who travels the world, inevitably picking up more and more languages along the way.

Taggart's true passion became learning languages after she realized the incredible connections with people that it fostered. Now she just can't get enough of it. Although it's taken time, she has acquired vast knowledge on the best and fastest ways to learn languages. But the truth is, she is driven simply by her motive to build exceptional links and bonds with others.

She is inspired everyday by the individuals she meets across the globe. For her, there's simply not anything as rewarding as practicing languages with others because she gets to make friends with people from all that come from a variety of cultures. This, in turn, has broadened her mind and thinking more than she would have ever imagined it could.

Of course, as a result of her constant travels, Taggart has become an expert on planning trips and making the most of time spent out of what she calls her "base" town. She jokes that she's practically at the nomad status now, but she's more content to live that way.

She knows how to live on a manageable budget weather she's in Paris or Phnom Penh. She knows how to seek out the adventures and thrills, no doubt, lying in wait at any city she visits. She knows that reflection on each every experience is significant if she wants to grow as a traveler and student of the world's cultures.

Because of this, Taggart chooses to share her understanding of languages and travel so that others, too, can experience the same life-altering benefits she has.

10004807R00061

Printed in Great Britain
by Amazon.co.uk, Ltd.,
Marston Gate.